Praise for *From Concept to Consumer*

"If you are an inventor or developer with a great idea for a product and the need to get it manufactured and distributed, this is the book for you. Here, Phil Baker reveals the valuable lessons he has learned from his many years of developing products for himself and others, getting them designed and manufactured, sometimes in the United States, sometimes in Asia. The discussion of Asian outsourcing is especially strong. 'The advantage is now to the swift and the creative, rather than the big,' says Baker, 'but to get that advantage you'll need to go to Asia.' Sound daunting? Don't worry; this book is a delightful tour of the virtues and dangers of outsourcing. If you want to get your product produced, this book is essential reading."

—Don Norman, Nielsen Norman Group, Author, *The Design of Future Things*

"I've known and admired Phil for years and to this day, I keep learning about significant products that I didn't know he had a hand in bringing to market. He's seen it all and done it all—and in this highly readable, immensely practical book, he tells all."

—Harry McCracken, Former Editor-in-Chief, *PC World*

"Phil Baker's book should be required reading for any entrepreneur as well as successful companies planning new products because they will gain important insight into what it takes to deliver new and innovative products in a digital age in which consumers demands, tastes, and desires often change overnight."

—Tim Bajarin, President, Creative Strategies, Inc.

"Phil Baker combines a long-earned knowledge of product design, manufacturing, and marketing to give us an insider's look at how a company or entrepreneur turns an idea into a real-world product. Ideas are easy, he observes, but creating something people want to buy is a complicated business, with many tradeoffs and difficult choices. He's been there, done that, and it shows."

—Dan Gillmor, Director, Knight Center for Digital Media Entrepreneurship, Kauffman Professor of Digital Media Entrepreneurship, Walter Cronkite School of Journalism & Mass Communication, Arizona State University

" Few people in the consumer electronics industry are as uniquely qualified as Phil to serve as a guide between idea and product. Even if you're not making a gadget, *From Concept to Consumer* offers an insightful and increasingly relevant look into a very different kind of project management. It's well worth the read if you want to build something people love."

—Ryan Block, Former Editor-in-Chief, *Engadget* and Cofounder, GDCT

"Phil Baker is one of those people whose career has spanned a generation of personal technology, and he's seen it all, from the design labs of California to the factory floors of Guangzhou. This book distills his experience in a highly readable guide to the ins and outs of getting a product to market, and the practical advice he offers will save many an entrepreneur from months and millions of dollars of pain. Anyone with a product in development or in their head should read it before they take another step."

—Jeremy Wagstaff, Technology Columnist and Blogger

"Phil Baker is one of the world's best minds in the consumer technology products industry. His keen insight and real-world understanding of product design, development, production, and marketing comes from years of experience versus from someone who has only 'studied' the consumer technology products market."

—Andy Abramson, CEO, Comunicano

FROM
CONCEPT
TO
CONSUMER

FROM
CONCEPT
TO
CONSUMER

PHIL
BAKER

To Asim,
Thanks for your years
of friendship.
Best Regards,
Phil
August 10, 2013

HOW TO
TURN
IDEAS INTO
MONEY

Vice President, Publisher: Tim Moore
Associate Publisher and Director of Marketing: Amy Neidlinger
Series Editor: Stewart Emery
Editorial Assistant: Myesha Graham
Development Editor: Russ Hall
Operations Manager: Gina Kanouse
Digital Marketing Manager: Julie Phifer
Publicity Manager: Laura Czaja
Assistant Marketing Manager: Megan Colvin
Cover Designer: Pentagram
Managing Editor: Kristy Hart
Project Editor: Chelsey Marti
Copy Editor: Geneil Breeze
Proofreader: Kathy Ruiz
Senior Indexer: Cheryl Lenser
Compositor: Bumpy Design
Manufacturing Buyer: Dan Uhrig

© 2009 by Pearson Education, Inc.
Publishing as FT Press
Upper Saddle River, New Jersey 07458

FT Press offers excellent discounts on this book when ordered in quantity for bulk purchases or special sales. For more information, please contact U.S. Corporate and Government Sales, 1-800-382-3419, corpsales@pearsontechgroup.com. For sales outside the U.S., please contact International Sales at international@pearson.com.

Company and product names mentioned herein are the trademarks or registered trademarks of their respective owners.

Printed in the United States of America

First Printing October 2008

ISBN-10: 0-13-713747-8
ISBN-13: 978-0-13-713747-3

Pearson Education LTD.
Pearson Education Australia PTY, Limited.
Pearson Education Singapore, Pte. Ltd.
Pearson Education North Asia, Ltd.
Pearson Education Canada, Ltd.
Pearson Educatión de Mexico, S.A. de C.V.
Pearson Education—Japan
Pearson Education Malaysia, Pte. Ltd.

Library of Congress Cataloging-in-Publication Data
Baker, Phil, 1943-
  From concept to consumer : how to turn ideas into money / Phil Baker.
    p. cm.
  ISBN 0-13-713747-8 (hbk. : alk. paper) 1. New products. 2. Product management. I. Title.
  HF5415.153B35 2009
  658.5'75--dc22
                    2008020661

For Jane, Karen, Dan, Holly, Kyan, and Clive

Contents

Acknowledgments

Writing this book is something I had thought about for a long time, but it was my wife, Jane, who persuaded me that I had a story to tell. Jane has been my unofficial editor for my weekly technology columns that I have been writing for many years for the *Daily Transcript*, San Diego's daily business paper. She also helped edit this book and made a considerable contribution to it, as well.

I'm also grateful to Reo Carr, the former Managing Editor of the *Transcript*, who persuaded me to write a weekly column, and to Bob Loomis, the *Transcript*'s Publisher who has been supportive and encouraging. I'm appreciative to Stewart Emery, a friend of 20 years and an accomplished author and business consultant, who guided me in this adventure. Thanks also to Tim Moore, Vice President and Publisher for FT Press, and Russ Hall, my editor, both of whom provided lots of good advice along the way. Instrumental in taking this book from manuscript to consumer have been Amy Neidlinger, Julie Phifer, Gina Kanouse, Laura Czaja, Megan Colvin, and Chelsey Marti.

I've relied on a number of friends and associates with specific expertise to review my manuscripts and provide advice and counsel. They include Jason Brook, Robert Brunner, Liam Casey, Martin Cooper, James Fallows, Chen Huang, Brett Johnson, Don Norman, Ray Oliver, Larry Reich, John Tang, Ken Wirt, and Louis Woo. I've also learned much over the years from several friends, each with entire careers spent in consumer retailing, Giles Bateman, Ryan Cyr, and John Rehfeld.

I'm also grateful to Richard Lee, Chairman of Inventec Corporation, who introduced me to the Taiwan ODM industry and, by his example, showed me how a company can serve the needs of its customers, employees, and shareholders, without compromising any of them.

I'm thankful to my daughter, Karen, and son, Dan, who never complained while I traveled during much of my career, and, in spite of my absence (or perhaps because of it) turned out so great. Karen also provided advice in the consumer marketing discussion, her area of expertise. Last, but not least to my mother, Barbara, who always encouraged me to take on new challenges and my late father, Louis, who I know would have enjoyed reading the book.

About the Author

Phil Baker has been involved in all aspects of product development for the consumer technology market for his entire career, with extensive experience in leveraging Asian companies for cost-effective and fast-to-market product development and manufacturing. He has a strong and varied background in business and product strategy in the high-technology sector.

Phil has played key roles in developing the innovative flagship technologies and products of many leading companies, including Apple, Seiko, Polaroid, Atari, Polycom, Proxima, Think Outside, and others. He cofounded Think Outside, the company that created one of the most popular PDA accessories ever, the Stowaway folding keyboard.

He received a B.S. in physics from Worcester Polytechnic Institute, an M.S. in engineering from Yale University, an M.B.A. from Northeastern University, and holds more than 30 patents.

Phil currently consults to companies in the United States and Asia in product, business, and market development and writes the technology column for the *San Diego Daily Transcript*. Phil was recipient of the 2005 Robert H. Goddard Alumni Award from WPI for Outstanding Professional Achievement and was the San Diego Ernst & Young Entrepreneur of the Year for Consumer Products in 2001. He resides with his wife, Jane, in Solana Beach, California. His website is www.philipgbaker.com; his columns are on his website; and his email is pbaker@gmail.com.

Preface

I've always been attracted to technology products and gadgetry. Throughout my career I've had the opportunity and good fortune to be associated with many defining consumer technology companies and products such as Polaroid's SX-70 camera, Apple's Newton MessagePad and PowerBooks, and many more.

I wrote this book to be able to share with readers what's involved in taking a concept and transforming it into a successful product, based on what I've seen and experienced for more than three decades.

One thing I've learned is that creating a successful product is much more than coming up with the idea; in fact, that's usually the easiest part. It's much more about what happens after. It involves a wide range of activities that bring together all sorts of disciplines, everything from engineering to product management to distribution to marketing. Each of these activities is much like a link in a chain. When one link fails, the entire endeavor can fail.

I thought this was an important story to be told and could find no other books that looked at all the activities in concert. While there are books on specific areas, such as engineering management, project management, and marketing, most of these are about processes, procedures, and theories, with only a few of them delving into real-life examples as experienced firsthand by the author. They don't convey the real-life, day-to-day issues, whose solutions often vary from conventional thinking. Those books are akin to what's taught in business school, while this book is more like the lab course that's never offered.

This book covers the new rules that have resulted from how quickly products are developed, their shorter life cycles, the use of outsourcing, and the Internet. All these factors have changed how things are now done. One of the biggest changes is the impact of China on product development and manufacturing and how it affects how we do things.

This book is intended not only for those involved in bringing out their own product, but also for those just curious about what's involved and how things work behind the scenes that rarely get exposed. This book will provide that along with some useful examples.

For entrepreneurs who work by themselves, as well as those involved in product related activities in both small and large companies, you'll have a better understanding of the steps to follow to be successful with your own products. You'll learn how to take advantage of new resources and new thinking. Plus you'll learn to ignore the naysayers who tell you not to buck the system and to just do it the way it's always been done. Most of all you'll have a better understanding of your options and what to expect.

I hope you enjoy reading the book as much as I enjoyed writing it.

CHAPTER I

New World, New Rules

The invention is often just 5% of all the factors for success.

I remember my first day at Polaroid in June 1967. I took the elevator to the third floor and then entered the secure area behind the frosted glass door with "Product Development" stenciled on it. Behind this door some of the world's great consumer products were being invented and engineered, and I would now become a part of it. The legend of Edwin Land, Polaroid's CEO, permeated the area. A modern-day Thomas Edison with hundreds of patents, Land had led Polaroid to become one of the great consumer product companies of all time with the invention of instant photography. I had always loved gadgets and consumer technology products, but had little idea what went on behind the scenes. Now I would have a chance to learn. It was a dream job, my first right out of graduate school.

One of the early products I worked on was Polaroid's first low-cost plastic instant camera, which took color pictures. Called the Colorpack II, it became a huge success, selling more than 5,000 cameras a day. My contribution was small. I designed a little periscope that lets you view the distance that the lens was set to when you looked into the viewfinder.

I watched the product come off the assembly line at the rate of one camera per minute and then a few weeks later walked into Lechmere Sales, a local discount store in Cambridge, Massachusetts, and saw throngs of people scrambling to buy one the first day it went on sale. This is one of the great rewards for those who develop consumer products—to take an idea and turn it into a product that millions will buy and enjoy.

I spent 16 years at Polaroid during its high growth years when it was a star of the high technology sector. I worked in a variety of positions, including engineering, quality control, manufacturing, marketing, product management, and business development, and also managed many of Polaroid's product development activities in Japan. Each was a new learning experience that took me down the road from concept to the consumer. I learned about concurrent engineering, the value of industrial design, the obsessions of patents, outsourcing, and designing high volume products. It was a solid foundation that has served me well.

Sadly, after 30 years of success, Polaroid was unable to react rapidly enough to the developments in digital photography. Rather than embrace it, they minimized its significance. By the time they realized its impact on their business, they were too late and declared bankruptcy in October 2001.

From that time I've worked on scores of products at companies with both familiar and strange names. The products include Polaroid cameras of all shapes and sizes for consumer and industry, Seiko's Smart Label Printer, pocket electronic dictionaries and gadgets, Apple's Newton MessagePad and PowerBook notebook computers, Proxima electronic projectors, Polycom's conferencing products, audio products, computer accessories, hardware, toys, handheld computers, and a full-size keyboard that folded up to fit in a pocket. I've accumulated about 30 patents along the way, some valuable and some useless.

I've continued to be fascinated with every aspect of product development. In fact, my California license plate reads PROD DEV (see Figure 1.1).

FIGURE 1.1 My license plate

Build It and They Won't Come

Coming up with the right idea, turning it into a product, and having it succeed in the marketplace is critical to a company's growth and survival. A company needs to be successful at it, but there's a lot more.

I used to believe that a product's success was based on how good the idea was. Build it and they will come. That's what most engineers are trained to believe (see Figure 1.2).

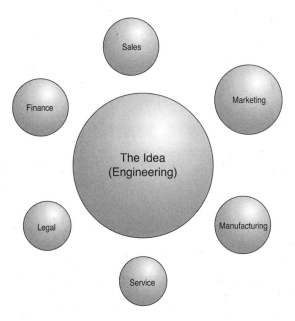

FIGURE 1.2 An engineer's viewpoint of a product's success

But the more products I worked on the more I realized that success comes from so many other factors. In fact, the invention is perhaps just 5% of all the factors for success. What are the others? You must get to market at just the right time with just the right product that sells for just the right price and still produces a profit. You need customers who are willing to buy. You need effective marketing and distribution that enable you to get the product into the right locations so people can see, try, and buy. Most important, you need good timing and just plain luck. If any of these links in the chain are broken, it can spell disaster.

All products begin with an idea or concept: a vision of something, a need to be solved, or an improvement to an existing device. At this stage there may be no idea of what the product will look like or how it will work. The first challenge is to take it from an amorphous idea to something that's real. The path from this concept stage to the consumer relies on a variety of disparate activities and decisions, each of which can result in success or failure.

Think Outside, a company that I co-founded, was formed on the premise of creating a full-size keyboard that could fold up and fit in a shirt pocket. My partner and I realized that with computing devices becoming smaller and our hands staying the same size, there needed to be a comfortable way to enter text. After trying a variety of design approaches, we settled on one that became the Stowaway keyboard for which the company became known (see Figure 1.3). But when we began we had only a rough idea of what we wanted to accomplish, without a practical solution.

FIGURE 1.3 The Stowaway keyboard

As difficult as it was to design and develop our product, there were many unexpected surprises ahead, some of which had nothing to do with the product idea, that nearly derailed the company.

And that was true with many of the products I worked on. Presentation Technologies, a company I co-founded in mid-1980s, invented a product that created 35mm slides for presentations from a personal computer. After a difficult but successful development effort, we encountered unexpected competition from new color printers, which made color overhead transparencies. This new technology was what's called a *disruptive change*, one that obliterated the 35mm presentation market.

I joined Proxima as vice president of engineering when it had only two competitors making electronic projectors that projected images from a computer onto a screen. Less than a year later there were three dozen competitors, plummeting margins from a healthy 40% to a tiny 16%. Polycom, another company I worked for, created a highly successful speakerphone for conference rooms. But the second product that I developed and managed for them, an overhead projector, fizzled. No one wanted it.

After working for and with many companies on many products, very little surprises me anymore. Rarely does a plan unfold as expected or as described in conventional books on product design and marketing.

Coming up with the clever idea may be the easiest part of all. Ideas are a dime a dozen. We all have them. "Why don't they make…" we say to ourselves. But thinking of a product is a long way from making it and succeeding. And having worked with smart people throughout my career, I can tell you that even the experts fail. Edwin Land failed with instant movies. Dean Kamen, another brilliant inventor, failed with the Segway, the self-balancing two-wheeled motorized scooter. And Steve Jobs failed with his Next computer.

There's no certainty that an idea will succeed. The Segway was an electrically powered vehicle that solved some of the most difficult engineering problems ever in a consumer product, including developing complex computer controlled gyros and motors to balance the two-wheeled device and keep it upright. It allowed users to lean forward, backward, or to the side to propel the vehicle forward and back and to steer. Yet the product was much too expensive, it ran into opposition from some communities who thought Segway users would run over pedestrians, and it turned out that there was little compelling need for the product. But just before it was announced, those who saw it, including corporate presidents, venture capitalists, and industry experts pronounced it so revolutionary, that it would result in new cities being built. The lessons learned are that no one can guarantee success, and even those that get it right sometimes also get it wrong at other times.

Developing successful products requires a team of people with the correct skills and the ability to work collaboratively. Some of the best-run projects have a strong project leader who manages and motivates the team. The biggest budget can't make up for a team that works at cross-purposes. I've seen some team members try to sabotage products they didn't like and others that would argue with the president for a product they believed in. People get passionate about products and don't always agree about what to put in and what to leave out. Some quit over it. Behind every product is usually a fascinating story. Even when you see a nearly perfect product, contentious team members likely were arguing behind the scenes. The decision to seal the battery into the iPhone put many within Apple at odds with Steve Jobs. Developing products is like making sausage. You don't always want to know what went into the product; it's better to just enjoy it.

I've also learned that success is not dependent on the size of a company. Those in small companies with limited resources can effectively compete and often have an advantage over Fortune 500 companies. While large companies have more engineers, extensive test labs, big marketing budgets, lawyers, huge sales forces, and a brand name, often their teams work less efficiently and make poorer decisions.

Why? They're attending more meetings, focusing on organizational issues, and often factoring their daily decisions on how they will affect their own careers, rather than on what's best for the business. Employees in small companies, on the other hand, know the company's success depends on a product's success and rarely waste their time on peripheral issues.

New Rules

Over the last decade product development, manufacturing, and marketing have undergone sweeping changes, creating new rules. Product life cycles have gone from years to months, manufacturing resources have moved from around the corner to around the world, and distribution has moved to the Internet and to a handful of big box stores as small owner-run stores have gone out of business.

Products have become more complex. We now have not just devices, but systems and platforms, such as Apple's iPod with its iTunes and online music store, and the Amazon Kindle, an electronic book with its own online bookstore and their Whispernet wireless network. With systems such as these you can make your purchase and be enjoying it within minutes.

Today we take an entirely new approach to how we do product development compared to a decade ago (see Figure 1.4). No longer can we afford the time to follow a sequential process, passing the product from engineering to manufacturing to marketing to sales. It's now done concurrently, with all the disciplines working together at the outset and contributing throughout the project. Not only is it faster, but it gets us better products.

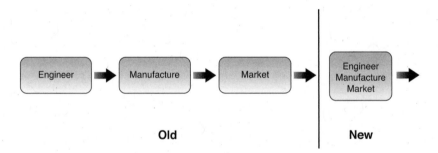

FIGURE 1.4 The old and new ways

In addition, companies need no longer do everything themselves, but instead use resources that didn't exist just a few years ago. More companies focus on doing what they do best and let other companies do for them what they do best. Worldwide resources give us huge new capabilities, whether we're a large or small company or even an individual. Developments in digital technology, the Internet, and high-speed communications allow us to use a manufacturer in Asia, a call center in India, and a designer in Europe.

Products are being designed using software that creates digital data to define every detail. This allows the engineer to send a digital file anywhere in the world in just seconds. It can go to a model maker in Taipei to create a prototype in a couple of days and to a toolmaker in China to build plastic tools used to produce the product in high volume. The same file can be fed into a machine to print out a three-dimensional model in an afternoon.

Any of a multitude of suppliers can be located in seconds on the Internet using Web sites such as Asian Sources and Alibaba. Fill out a single request form and it will be transmitted electronically to the relevant companies, who often respond within a few hours.

Advances made in the electronics industry now allow us to create products by assembling electronic building blocks like Legos. Companies with little electronics skill can quickly create sophisticated products.

Formerly, complex electro-mechanical consumer products took years to develop. Polaroid's SX-70 camera, their first to fold small enough to fit in a jacket pocket and use film that didn't need to be peeled apart, took more than five years to engineer.

There was little competition to be concerned about and the product would be on the market for many years to come, perhaps a decade or more.

Today the competition is much more intense, and products are revised and improved more frequently. Why? Because if you don't do it, your competitors will, and it's often the only way to maintain visibility in the crowded market.

Cell phone models, once lasting a year or two, are now being replaced in as little as three months. Some digital cameras and iPods are replaced or upgraded every six months.

For all these reasons we're forced to work at a more frantic pace. There's little time to conduct extensive market research and to go back and start over. Experience, intuition, and gut play a bigger role than ever. It's like running at a marathon pace just to stay in place.

Asia

The United States and Europe lost their competitive edge in building high technology, high volume consumer product development decades ago, and never developed the infrastructure needed to compete. The government's focus and investment were in defense technology while Asian companies and governments invested in consumer technology.

My first trip to Asia occurred more than 30 years ago when I was developing a slide copier at Polaroid called the Polaprinter. It was a product for industry and professionals that produced an instant color print from a 35mm slide. Polaroid, like other large companies at the time, had a serial process requiring the engineering design to be done before the manufacturing engineers would get involved. That meant a long process of design, manufacturing review, and redesign. I thought I'd be able to bring the product to market more quickly by using a small Japanese company, Sunpak, that had design and manufacturing skills for similar products.

Japan pioneered the use of teams with skills in both design and manufacturing. No passing a design back and forth, just one team to get it right the first time. Most Japanese engineers were trained in both design and manufacturing and could fulfill either role. They realized that a good design was one that also could be manufactured efficiently and it made them better at both jobs.

I didn't go to Japan for lower cost labor but to save money by getting to market more quickly. Many studies have been conducted since and have concluded that more profits come from entering the market sooner, even with the added costs of accelerated development. In the case of the Polaprinter, the bet paid off. We were in production within a year of beginning the design, much faster than most products.

Over the past three decades there's been a movement of technical proficiency, infrastructure, and manufacturing of consumer technology from Japan southwest to Taiwan, Singapore, Hong Kong, Korea, and China. Japan served as the example from which the other countries learned (see Figure 1.5).

FIGURE 1.5 Map of Asia

Japan is no longer competitive for manufacturing most consumer products, and many of the once small entrepreneurial companies have grown larger and become more bureaucratic over the years. Hong Kong developed its engineering and manufacturing skills to build technology products, but eventually shifted its priorities to focus on finance as its factories moved to China.

Currently Taiwan and Korea have some of the most technically advanced and highly educated workforces and have become homes to the most advanced notebook computer and mobile phone designers and manufacturers. But as their standard of living has risen to match ours, their labor costs have increased so that now, the manufacturing of many of their products has moved to China.

A majority of consumer technology products are currently being made in Southern China in the province of Guangdong, particularly around its capital city, Shenzhen (see Figure 1.6), near Hong Kong. Many of these factories are owned and run by their Taiwanese, Hong Kong, and other foreign owners. I've brought many products to be developed and manufactured to all of these countries over the past two decades but now focus mostly on China and Taiwan.

While cost was once the main reason, it's no longer the primary one for our building products in these countries. A bigger reason is to get the product to market more quickly and with fewer hassles than doing it in the United States or in Europe. Even as labor costs rise in China, it remains the best place to go. It's become almost a requirement to go there if you intend to compete in the consumer world. China has the resources and the infrastructure and is referred to as the manufacturer for the world for high tech consumer products.

FIGURE 1.6 Map of Southern China

But, as you'll discover in the pages of this book, going to Asia is not so easy and is fraught with risks and challenges. Many companies have only horror stories to report after trying to use China for development or manufacturing.

A number of products that I've brought to China have run into problems. Sometimes it seems the longer I work there the less I know. But that's because the area is expanding so rapidly. This book will take you through some of these experiences. I'll share with you what I learned, so, perhaps, you can avoid making the same mistakes.

CHAPTER 2

Just Do It

Be as innovative in the development process as in the invention process.

Innovation is not something that's confined to the product. I've always believed it was possible to bring the same level of creativity to the development process as well. Over the years I've searched for ways to speed up the time to market, reduce development costs, and avoid those common bureaucratic delays that occur, particularly in large companies. Why is this important? Because getting to market first with new technology provides a big competitive edge in establishing a brand and in maximizing profit.

Organizing for Rapid Development

Whether in a small company or large, I've found the use of small multidiscipline teams under the direction of a strong, enthusiastic, and capable product manager to be a highly effective way to get the product to market quickly. It's proven to be much more effective than using larger conventional functional organizations that typically perform each role in isolation of one another. Small focused teams are much more effective than large organizations because they communicate better, there's less bureaucracy, and decisions get made more quickly.

This approach worked well when I used it at Apple to develop the Newton MessagePad 110. I assembled a small team for the duration of the project, approximately ten months. Members were borrowed from functional organizations and became part of a matrix organization, as

illustrated in Figure 2.1. Once the product was completed, the members
either went back to their functional groups or joined another project
team. Each member of the team represented and spoke for one of the
key functional disciplines: engineering, industrial design, marketing,
finance, and manufacturing.

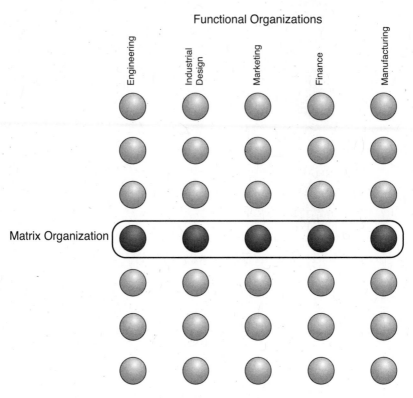

FIGURE 2.1 Matrix organization

Some team members were individual contributors, while others
represented a larger organization working behind the scenes on the
product. For example, a software manager on the team reported
on software issues and took back important information about the
project to the engineers. This served to keep everyone informed and
helped the software engineers understand how what they were doing
fit into the big picture.

THE APPLE NEWTON

The Apple Newton was one of the earliest and most advanced PDAs (personal digital assistants). It was essentially a powerful pocket-sized computer using an ARM processor that could be carried everywhere. It was designed to maintain a list of contacts and a calendar, as well as run a variety of applications including a word processor and spreadsheet. Its touch screen allowed access to a variety of innovative features such as moving text, capturing ink notes, handwriting recognition, and turning free-hand shapes into perfectly shaped objects. It could understand a written phrase such as "meet with Dan on Thursday at noon" and add the event to the calendar. The first model, the MessagePad 100, was made by Sharp in Japan and subsequent models, beginning with the MessagePad 110, were built by Inventec in Taiwan.

The Newton was sold from 1993–1998.

Because everyone had a better understanding of the entire project, it allowed each of them to see the importance and impact of their activities. It's in contrast to the way some companies operate, in which little importance is placed on communication between the functional groups who often work independently of one another and are unaware of how they impact the project.

The team approach was effective in bringing a broad perspective to critical decisions. It didn't foster decisions by committee; the engineers were still responsible for engineering decisions, and the marketing people for marketing decisions. But collaborating resulted in better decision-making and encouraged teamwork.

The team changed its composition over time as responsibilities ebbed and flowed from one area to the next. Finance was involved during the inception stage to help with budgets and contracts, and then phased out later.

Whenever a product is going to be made in Asia, I try to include the manufacturer as part of the team to leverage their knowledge. DFM, design for manufacturing, ensures the product uses the right components and is optimized for production in specific factories. Involving the manufacturer right from the beginning, usually by conference call or video call, as well as face-to-face visits ensured there was no need to go back later and make changes. Face-to-face visits were crucial not only to ensure that communication was clear, but also to set milestones and expectations. Knowing your customer is coming causes the factory to better prepare and be more attentive to your needs.

One example of how the team worked together involved a decision about whether to use AA or AAA rechargeable batteries to power the Newton MessagePad. AA batteries provided twice the battery life but also made the product bigger. The industrial designer on the team, Jony Ive (now senior vice president of industrial design at Apple), built a number of hard models of what the product might look like with the different-size batteries, while the engineers did an analysis to determine how frequently the two types of batteries would need to be charged. Marketing assessed the customer satisfaction issue versus the size. In the end we all agreed to use a design incorporating the AA batteries, primarily because Ive came up with a stunning design that effectively masked the added bulk.

Being involved meant everyone understood the facts behind the decision and avoided second-guessing later on. In short order, the members moved from thinking of themselves as borrowed members to being part of a close-knit, hard-working group. In fact, years later many of us still keep in touch and fondly remember those exciting times.

FIGURE 2.2 The Apple Newton MessagePad 110

How big a team do you need? While it varies by product, a team of five to ten people is ideal. That's small enough to work well and communicate effectively together, yet provides the diversity of resources needed to address almost any issue. The team developing the Newton MessagePad 110 had eight people—an electronics engineer, a software engineer, a mechanical engineer, a manufacturing/tooling engineer, a project manager, a project coordinator, a marketing manager, and an operations/business manager. On the other hand, the team that developed the Stowaway folding keyboard had five members—a mechanical engineer, a manufacturing/tooling engineer, an electronics engineer, a software engineer, and a marketing person. The mechanical engineer was also the project manager.

Get Customer Input

I'm a strong believer in getting customer feedback early in the development process. While it's not a substitute for good decision-making, getting this information is helpful to check the assumptions being made about the product and to ensure the product is not developed in total isolation nor is way off the mark. As the engineer, I was often so close to a product that it was hard to step back and look at it objectively. It's easy to develop tunnel vision while being immersed in the design work. Often when I've had others look at a product, they'd ask a question totally off the wall, but in doing so, it caused me to look at something in a new way.

Speaking with potential customers helps product developers to learn which features are most important, understand the pricing sensitivity, and see how the product would be used. I often gained an entirely new insight in watching someone use a product for the first time. However, customer feedback is less useful if it's for an entirely new type of product, as this requires them to use their imagination to understand it.

I've found the value of the information I get to be dependent on what I ask and how I ask the questions. Asking "Would you buy the product for $150?" is far less useful than asking customers to specify at what prices you would not buy, maybe buy, and definitely buy the product, or to write down the amount on a piece of paper when part of a larger group.

Still, many truly great products have succeeded in spite of conventional wisdom or an expert's dislike of it. Great products are often the result of a visionary leader who looks at a new way to do something, quite apart from how it's been done before. Conventional marketing testing is far less useful in these cases.

When Apple came out with the iPhone it was the first smartphone to rely totally on a touch screen keyboard instead of physical keys such as those used on a Blackberry. Most experts and technology reviewers, myself included, thought this was a serious deficiency. Typing on glass? You have to be kidding! If you did a customer survey you'd get the same reaction.

But Steve Jobs and his engineers recognized that this feature enabled the use of a large display, valuable for many of the other functions such as Web browsing. In these other modes when the keyboard was not needed it simply disappeared, something a real keyboard could not do. The huge success of the iPhone proved Apple's decision to be correct, at least for its primary audience.

When we wanted feedback on our Stowaway keyboard we met with Logitech, one of the world's largest keyboard marketing companies, to ask their opinion. While they marveled at the design and ingenuity, they told us the product would need to retail for under $40 to be successful. They were judging the product by its utility as a keyboard, and most of theirs, although much larger, sold in that price range. They failed to recognize the new uses for such a product, the emotional appeal of the Stowaway, and the magic of transforming a pocket-size object to a full-size keyboard. We went on to sell more than two million units, most at a $100 retail. Perhaps it's hard to know what could be when you think you know what is.

The lesson in all this is that customer feedback can be useful, if for nothing more than confirming you're on the right track. But it's best used for evolutionary products and less so for radically new designs.

Leveraging Outside Resources

Leveraging is a powerful tool for accelerating product development. It means doing what you do best and letting others do what they do best. Using outside resources reduces the need for permanent ones. It makes it easier to expand and contract, and avoids adding fixed overhead costs. This applies throughout the project, including everything from the way the product is designed to how the product is manufactured, delivered, and sold. It's the opposite of NIH, not invented here, an unfortunate tradition in many companies that insist they can and should do everything themselves.

Fortunately, NIH is now dead in progressive companies. In fact, one of the huge shifts over the last 20 years has been that companies outsource their work to others, even to competitors. Enlightened companies rarely are resistant to work with others if it can help them do something better, faster, or cheaper. While this may be a more recent phenomenon in the United States and Europe, it's been going on in Japan for decades and is one of the reasons for the Japanese being so effective at bringing products to market.

I first saw this during one of my visits to Japan when dozens of companies introduced video cassette recorders (VCRs) all within a time span of a few months. A VCR was an incredibly complex product with hundreds of mechanical parts that by comparison make a mechanical watch look simple.

I wondered how so many companies could create such complex devices so quickly. As it turned out, things were less than they seemed. The VCR companies all sourced the innards—the transport mechanism, the magnetic head assembly, and some of the electronics—from the same suppliers, each specializing in designing and producing specific parts and assemblies. The VCR companies didn't insist on doing everything themselves. In fact, they could not have done so profitably. This has become a popular form of leveraging, using companies that specialize in doing a part of your product well so you need not reinvent something from scratch.

A company need not surrender its core competency or "soul" by doing this. Hewlett-Packard, one of the first to market laser printers, built its product based on technology from Canon. Hewlett-Packard has led in this category ever since and used it to expand to other printing technologies, many developed internally.

Apple uses outside resources to design some of the more complex elements of its computers. For example, some of the mechanical hinges on notebooks that need to work reliably for tens of thousands of cycles are designed by a company that specializes in such mechanisms. While using these resources is often more expensive, it's easily justified by reducing time to market and by having a reliable design based on the outside company's years of experience in a specialized area.

Leveraging can also be used in other ways. A number of years ago one of my project teams was developing a product that needed a battery compartment with a snap-on battery cover. Something simple, right? Actually it's often a weak point of a design. The batteries need to always make contact even when the product is shaken vigorously; an interruption of power in some devices, even if only for a fraction of a second, can be a problem. Thus the designs of the springs, contacts, foam pad, and the confinement of the batteries are very important.

The team's mechanical engineer was eager to develop his own unique design. After all, engineers are trained to be creative. But I asked him first to examine several Japanese phones that had similar battery compartments and had been on the market for many years. I suggested he incorporate the best of these designs into our product. After all, by this time the borrowed design must be nearly perfect. Why start over with a new design that would add more time, and need to be tested and likely refined?

Multiply this by a half dozen design elements and you can see how doing this can shorten the schedule and reduce risk. By the way, I don't condone violating patents, but features like this are rarely patentable; some of the phone's design was likely borrowed from others. I like to say that if you use the first design you look at, that's copying; but if you take the best of several designs you examine, that's applied research. The smartest companies don't care who does the design, just that it's done well and timely.

Remembering That Less Is More

One of the challenges of designing a product is deciding what features to include. If you ask, most engineers want to provide a product that does as much as possible, and more than the competition. But more is sometimes less, and less is sometimes more. More features mean more development time, more risks, more cost, harder to use, added support costs, and often not a better product.

The Palm PDA, shown in Figure 2.3 and created by Jeff Hawkins, one of the company's founders, was perceived as a computerlike device that would be simple to use. To gain that simplicity it was as important to know what to leave out as much as what to include. If he had tried to please everyone, the product would likely have turned out to be as complex as a computer.

A more recent example is a simple-to-use pocket video camera called The Flip, also shown in Figure 2.3, that sells for $150. It's pocket size, takes 60 minutes of video, and plugs directly into a computer's USB port to automatically transfer the files. It needs no software disks or cables and uses AA batteries, even eliminating a charger. The results are as good as videos from cameras three times the price.

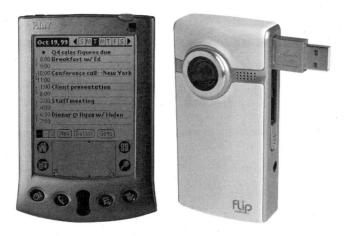

FIGURE 2.3 Palm V and The Flip video camera

I'm surprised by how few still understand the value of simplicity. I recently read a review of a new pocket-size digital still camera. I know the camera well, and it's a joy to use. I carry one everywhere and can quickly pull it out of my pocket to grab a candid shot. Yet the review criticized it for not having manual controls to adjust exposure and focus. That's not what the camera is about. Adding such features invariably gets in the way of spontaneous picture taking. Pull out the camera to grab a quick picture, and there will be times when the settings were left on manual and you'll miss the shot.

Many reviewers of products for technology magazines, Web sites, and blogs contribute to this problem. They rate a product by how feature-rich it is. Ease of use is rarely an issue because the reviewers are adept at using almost any product, no matter how complex it is. And because the product engineers and marketing people read these magazines, that's the criteria they design to.

Putting unnecessary features in a product not only complicates its use, but also lengthens the development time and adds to the design and testing requirements, not to mention increasing cost and follow-up customer support. When developing a product, I'll incorporate a borderline feature if it doesn't add much more cost or complexity, if it's easy to understand, if the product looks or works better with it, and if including it will increase sales. I'll leave it out if it's unlikely to increase sales, it's a feature few will care about, or if it adds to the cost, risk, or development time.

Don't Get Hung Up with Perfection

How do you know when the product is good enough? Some will argue that it needs to be nearly perfect before being released for sale. It needs to have all the features, each has to work perfectly, the product has to be thoroughly tested, and every weakness addressed. After all, don't you just get one chance to get it right?

That's less the case today. Of course the product needs to be reliable, meaning it should work as expected, and the manufacturing quality should be high, meaning the unit-to-unit variability should be small. But one of the most important things I've learned is, after agonizing over a product for months or even a year or more during the development and manufacturing, and being so close to it, you really don't know the product as well as you think you do. Not until it gets into the hands of customers do you really get to understand your product and learn of its deficiencies.

The Polaroid SX-70 camera went through years of development, but not until it got into the hands of users did the design team realize how serious a deficiency it had. Actually a few knew, including myself, but those closest to the project failed to grasp its importance.

I was running Polaroid's test labs during the year prior to the SX-70's introduction. As part of testing the camera using a variety of first-time users, I found many had difficulty accurately focusing using the

SLR-like matte screen. Dr. Land designed the camera so the image would appear out of a fog and come into sharp focus as the focus wheel was turned. He wanted to replicate how the image would emerge on the actual film as it was developing.

However, the focus was also used to set the flash exposure, and the exposure was much more sensitive to getting a precise focus. As a result about 30% of all flash pictures were unacceptable, being either too dark or completely washed out. I quickly put together my findings and thought it would be catastrophic if the product went to market. I took the findings to Dr. Land's assistant and the SX-70 design team, and showed them my conclusions. They all politely thanked me but said they had been working on the product for years and hadn't seen similar results. If it turned out to be a problem, we'd just have to teach customers to do a better job focusing. Pure denial.

But my analysis had shown that the focusing system was not capable of even an expert getting good results. I naively thought the company's burden was on my shoulders, although few others seemed to see things as dire.

After a few weeks of experimenting, I came up with a solution. It involved modifying the focus screen in a way to provide a split-image focusing aide that quadrupled the accuracy, sufficient to get good exposures. I added it to a camera, tested it, and it worked. I showed it to Land's assistant, and he seemed impressed. But he said I could not show this to anyone or I could be fired. The visible focusing element went against Dr. Land's vision of the image coming out of the fog, and if Land heard about someone working contrary to this, that person's job might be in danger.

I had done all I could do. I identified the problem and then found a solution, but others were not willing to recognize that there was a problem, at least not just yet.

The product came to market a few weeks later, with the only negative news being that it had a serious exposure problem, but was otherwise well reviewed in a hugely successful PR campaign which included Dr. Land and his SX-70 appearing on the cover of *Life* magazine.

A month after the product went on sale I got a call to go to Dr. Land's office with my prototype. He said to me that he heard that I had a solution to the exposure problem and asked me to show and explain it to him. He looked into the camera and tried it out, saying nothing. After 5 minutes he told his assistant that we would incorporate this into the SX-70 as a running change, but locate it below the center of the image so as not to make it too noticeable. He congratulated me for my efforts and said we would have to find another solution that would eliminate the visible focus aid entirely.

The new fix was phased in a few months later. However, Dr. Land was still unhappy that his original vision had to be abandoned, so a year later he introduced the first camera to have an auto-focusing system, eliminating the need for my focus aid. To this day, one of my most memorable patents is as co-inventor with Dr. Land for a focus aid located below the center of the picture.

What this demonstrates is that those close to a product, even one of the most famous inventors of all time, often can't see or accept the flaws in an invention, or perhaps, more appropriately, his baby. However, once forced to do so, a brilliant inventor such as Edwin Land turned a defect into a challenge and used it to spur further innovation. But even for him to see the problem, he first had to get it into the customers' hands to be convinced.

I recently was working with a client who was developing a Bluetooth cellphone headset that offered unheard of audio performance. Both directions of the conversation were crisp and clear with none of the typical background noise, quite an accomplishment because Bluetooth headsets historically have a high return rate due to poor audio quality. While this product had great audio performance at both ends of the conversation, when the phone and headset were close to one another, performance fell off faster than with conventional models as the separation increased to a few feet or even less if blocked by the body. It was a necessary compromise to obtain the high performance. What it meant was that if a phone was placed in the user's left pants pocket and the earpiece was in his right ear, there might be static as the signal passed through the body.

A debate raged within the company about this weakness. The marketing director said the product was not good enough to sell. The designer thought the product was better than anything else available. But not until the product got in the hands of a few hundred customers was the answer found. To quell the debate I did what either the marketing director or the designer could have done, but perhaps found difficult to do after staking out their positions. I simply called a representative sample of the early buyers and asked them to rate a number of items including the performance. They overwhelmingly praised the product for its audio quality and, while some recognized the shorter range, none found it to be a big deal; they just moved the phone a little closer. What's the lesson? You learn most about the product after it gets into the hands of the customers. You can guess, debate, and hypothesize, but you really don't know until then.

A funny thing often happens when the product is nearly done and ready to ship, even after considerable internal testing. Some get nervous. They want to make some last-minute changes and delay the introduction. It's like stage fright.

But it's best to get the product out, get some feedback, and learn from the experience. In fact, you do have second chances nowadays. With rapid development you can make changes quickly. Customers now expect it. They're tolerant of it and have been conditioned to put up with a few problems as early adopters. A visit to the chat boards discussing new technology products will show many examples of issues encountered with newly released products.

My advice is to design and manufacture the best product you can within your time and budget constraints and then get it out to the public. They will tell you which refinements you need to make, either as revisions or in your follow-on products. But also be sensitive to your customers' needs by having a liberal return policy for the early adopters. Offer discounts or trade-ins on future upgraded models and give full refunds to unsatisfied customers. This way, despite any problems they encounter with your product, early adopters will be your advocates and not your detractors.

CHAPTER 3

The Basics of Development

A successful product design is one that meets the needs
of its customers at a price they can afford.

Developing a product is an adventure filled with ups and downs, excitement and disappointments. It's a marathon race to work as quickly as possible, but still do a thorough job creating a product that works well and is commercially successful. It's a blend of research, engineering, marketing, and intuition. It's about balancing features, cost, and time to market while never quite knowing what will be your competition once you get done and what obstacles you might run into along the way.

The development process involves a series of steps of defining, designing, and engineering; testing and validating and finally manufacturing. But development cannot be done in isolation; it needs to be done considering the market requirements, product specs, schedule, and the product's cost. There's little value in developing a product that few want or can afford or is introduced when the window of opportunity has passed. No matter how well engineered, no product is truly successful if it doesn't meet the needs of those willing to pay for it.

This chapter describes the development process, along with the four key elements that are so integrally tied to it: the market, the specification, the schedule, and the cost; in other words, who, what, when, and how much.

Development

It can take as little as a few months or as long as several years to develop a product. The time it takes depends on how well the product is defined at the start, the complexity of the product, the size of the development team, how many changes are made along the way, and how well the project is managed.

Look at a new high-tech product on the shelf of a store, such as an iPod, and realize that it didn't get there without a lot of effort from many people who may have begun planning years before. While it now works well and is beautiful looking, it went through a long process to get there.

First the product was conceived, perhaps as a sketch, and then, after defining its appearance, it was engineered, squeezing all the components into an enclosure as small as possible. The controls were created to provide the needed functions, and solid, nonworking models were built to better visualize the size and weight. Outside suppliers were involved to supply the touch wheel, the display, and the chips.

Finally working models made up of circuit boards and components were built to test and refine the design. Months of work were done, in both the hardware and firmware (software that is part of the device). Many changes were made along the way, because some features didn't work as expected. Engineering prototypes or hand-assembled working units, called breadboards, were built and tested again. Finally tooling was made, and thousands of units were built with production-quality parts. They were tested in real life for many months before going through more changes and finally going into production. Eventually products were assembled on a huge production line, tested at each stage, and then packaged and shipped, finally reaching the store shelves.

I remember on numerous occasions sitting with an early prototype of a product in my hands that took weeks to build and barely functioned. It was difficult to imagine such a fragile thing could ever be produced in huge volumes that would work reliably.

I've created a visual map of the development process showing many of the key development activities that occur during the process from concept to production (see Figure 3.1). The map provides a clear picture of the entire process from beginning to end. You'll see a lot of parallel activities rather than a string of serial ones. Activities are begun assuming others in progress will be successful. Sometimes a backup design is done in parallel in case the primary one fails.

What the map doesn't show is some of the anxiety and pressures that team members face day in and day out, including difficult decisions such as starting a design over or making a large financial commitment to buy parts for a design that's not even finished. But somehow in the end everything usually comes together.

A typical development process can be divided into several phases:

> Phase 1: Concept Design
>
> Phase 2: Design Development
>
> Phase 3: Detailed Development
>
> Phase 4: Preproduction
>
> Phase 5: Production

This can be a rigorous process that often involves reviews at the end of each phase attended by senior executives. Companies often add gates or criteria that must be met to move from one phase to the next, and require executive approval for any changes to the product.

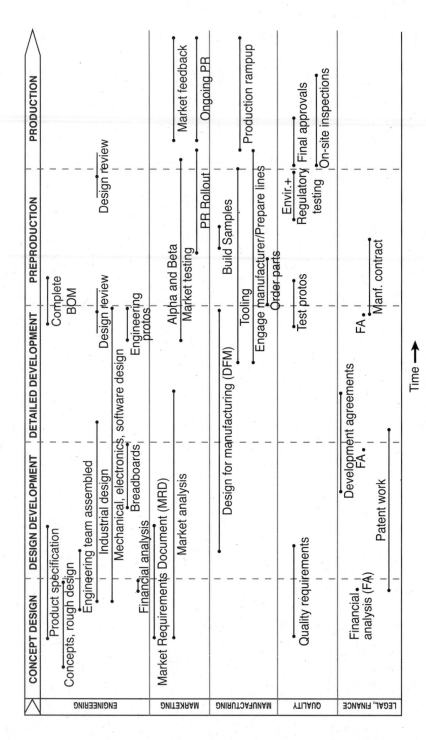

FIGURE 3.1 Product development map

Phase I: Concept Design

This investigation phase takes a fledgling idea and brings it to something more formative. The concept is firmed up, the initial mechanical and electronic designs are defined, and the industrial design begins with some sketches. A variety of design approaches are examined, narrowed down and tested to select the most appropriate ones. Resources are identified, and a team begins to be assembled.

A product specification and a market requirements document (MRD) are begun that describe the product and the market requirements. A financial analysis of the entire project is done to estimate the size of the investment and potential return.

The cost of developing a product varies widely, but generally ranges from a few hundred thousand dollars to several million dollars. Up to this point there's been only a small investment made compared to what's to come.

Phase 2: Design Development

An engineering team is assembled and begins to develop the mechanical and electrical designs, and the software. The industrial design is developed and incorporated into the overall design. Breadboards, are built and tested, circuits are assembled, and software concepts are created.

A breadboard of an iPhone might be the size of a cookie sheet that has a circuit board, display, radios, antennas, power source, and connectors mounted on a flat panel that allows it to be moved around.

As the product evolves and circuits are compressed onto tiny chips, the breadboard will move closer to resembling the final product. Nonworking models are built to help the team visualize and assess the appearance, size, and shape. Mechanisms are created and tested, components are identified, materials are selected, and a bill of materials begins to be developed listing all the parts of the product. A preliminary cost estimate is made and a manufacturer is selected.

Phase 3: Detailed Development

The product design is further developed, almost to completion. Detailed drawings, schematics, and digital files are refined that take into consideration how the product will be manufactured and utilize the actual components that will be used in production. The first prototype that looks, works, and is constructed from the actual parts will be hand-built, emulating the design that will be used in mass production.

It's then evaluated for function, appearance, and marketability. Materials and finishes are chosen. Design reviews are conducted to go over all the engineering details. Another financial and marketing assessment is conducted, before committing the tens or hundreds of thousands of dollars to tooling, to be sure the product still is viable in the market and the economic assumptions valid. Tooling begins.

Phase 4: Preproduction

The preproduction phase refines the design based on what's learned from building and testing the prototypes during Phase 3 and incorporates that into the final design. The bill of materials (a list of parts) and assembly drawings are finalized. Tolerances of all the critical parts are analyzed, and a thorough review of the design is conducted with the manufacturer. Orders are placed for the components, such as the display and chips, in quantities to support volume production. Preproduction samples are built and tested for performance, durability, and regulatory requirements.

Phase 5: Production

Tooling is completed. Parts are made just as they will be for production and used to build small quantities of the product, often several hundred. These are as close to production products as possible and will be used for final testing, assembly, and marketing, but can't be sold. It's the first time that enough units are built to assess how manufacturing variations impact the performance.

The products are then tested for environmental extremes—from severe cold to hot and humid temperatures. They are dropped, subjected to shock and vibration to simulate being shipped, and subjected to rough usage. Moving parts are repetitively cycled for thousands of cycles to simulate years of use in just a few weeks. Samples are submitted for regulatory requirements such as UL (Underwriters Laboratories), FCC (Federal Communications Commission), and CE (European conformity). The product is provided to potential customers to use and report back their findings, a process called *beta testing*. Beta testing can be a huge project, depending on the product and the company's needs. It's the last time and best way before the product is released for sale to learn about a products' user acceptability, performance, and even the clarity of the instruction manual.

Meanwhile, the assembly line is being prepared, assembly operators are being trained, and work instructions are being created that describe each step of assembly, adjustment, and testing, all in preparation for building large volumes of the product.

Production begins.

Marketing

It's always best to know where you're heading before you start your engines. That's the purpose of clearly defining what the product is, whom it's for, and what's needed to succeed in the market. It's a critical input into the development effort. Although there's a full chapter on marketing later in the book, it needs to be considered as part of the development, as well.

Having a clear and concise description at the outset makes it a lot easier to develop the product. Committing the details to words better defines the product and forces some basic decisions of what's in and what's out, what's important and what's not. It also helps to communicate the details of the product to all those involved and to establish a baseline for the entire development activity. But changes will still occur along the way based on the market, technology, and competition.

Every product should have an MRD, a market requirements document that, in just a few pages, describes the product and how it relates to the market. It provides product goals, sets priorities, and becomes a catalyst for discussion between the marketing and development teams about what's important. Had one of the original Newton's top priorities not been handwriting recognition, things might have turned out better. When it became a problem, engineering and marketing should have reduced its importance as a feature and stressed other features instead of just hoping for the best.

The MRD includes brief comments on each of the following items:

1. Product description.

2. How the product works.

3. Why the product is needed.

4. Product features.

5. If software is included, what it does and how it works.

6. Who the product is for.

7. How big the market is for the product.

8. What the competition is for the product and how it compares.

9. Where the product will be sold.

10. What price the product needs to sell for.

11. What profit margins are required for the product.

12. How the product will be serviced and supported.

13. The estimate of the product's sales volume.

Estimating Sales

Estimating the sales is important because it impacts how the product is designed and manufactured. High-volume products utilize more tooling, requiring more investment, so that parts can be made more cheaply. Lower-volume products are designed to reduce the need for tooling, but the individual parts will be more costly. (*Tooling* is the machinery used to automatically replicate a large number of parts instead of making them individually by hand. One of the most common types is tooling to mold plastic parts.)

Another important need for getting accurate sales estimates is planning for sufficient manufacturing capacity. The success of a new high-volume product can often create a demand that outstrips the manufacturer's or a component company's capacity. Plans need to be made in advance for bringing up additional assembly lines or finding additional suppliers.

Developing an accurate sales forecast is difficult and is often an educated guess, because it depends on so many variables such as cost, competition, and how and where a product is sold. Make estimates from several different perspectives. Look at the market size for a product, the total sales expected of all products in the category at the time of introduction. How will your product sell compared to the others? Is it competitive enough to capture 5% of the market or 30%? Remember, it takes time to create awareness, and even when someone becomes aware of your product, the buying decision may stretch out for months. It took ten years for the first 50% of the potential market to purchase a DVD player.

Sales data is often available from market research companies such as NPD (www.npd.com), which compiles monthly sales volumes of consumer electronic products by category based on surveying sales outlets.

For the Stowaway, we calculated our estimates two ways: comparing to one other product and from the ground up. One company was selling an undersized-nonfolding keyboard. We estimated that ours would sell at about 10 times their volume because it was a much better product and was being sold under the Palm brand using their worldwide distribution. We also estimated sales by assuming an attach rate (the percentage of new Palm PDA buyers who would buy a keyboard) of 5% to 7%. While that turned out to be accurate in the first year, as competition came in and Palm introduced lower priced PDAs to a broader market, the attach rate dropped to 3% in the third year.

Product Specs

Just as an MRD defines the product from the user's perspective, a product specification describes details about the product from a technical perspective.

It includes details on each of these items with more technical detail than the MRD:

1. Description of the product, how it works, and how it is used.

2. Description of the controls, switches, lights, displays, and ports.

3. If there's software, what it does and how does it work.

4. The physical attributes: size, weight, and so on.

5. The environmental conditions the product must work in. This includes high temperature, low temperature, humidity, and so on.

6. The physical conditions it's subjected to and in which it must work. This includes how high it can be dropped and the shock and vibration levels, both outside and inside its packaging.

7. Quality requirements. How long it lasts, how many and what types of defects are allowed, and how the is product tested.

8. The regulatory agencies and requirements the product must meet.

The specification is the document that communicates the product's technical requirements to the engineers and the manufacturer. It becomes part of the manufacturing agreement, and influences how the product is to be designed and built.

For example, a product that needs to withstand high temperatures and sustain a drop from several feet in height will determine the types of materials to be used and how the product will be constucted and assembled.

An initial version of both the specification and the MRD need to be available early in Phase 2, Design Development, providing the product requirements for the rest of the development process.

Schedule

When the product comes to market can make the difference between success and failure. The schedule is developed early in the process under certain assumptions of what needs to be done and how long it will take. A product introduction is often timed to an important trade show or industry event where it can be introduced to as wide an audience as possible. These events provide great visibility to small companies with small marketing budgets. They can result in press coverage and introductions to potential customers and marketing partners.

Rarely does a schedule include the unexpected delays that are difficult to anticipate. The most common things that impact a schedule are unexpected problems, such as a design that doesn't work and needs more time to fix, a component that's late, or more time needed to get the software and hardware to work together. This is an area where using a little creativity can have a big impact. (And where being a worrier can also help.) If the product relies on the success of a risky design or a unique component for it to succeed, then carry along a second design in parallel. The extra cost is usually well worth it to stay on schedule. Of course, adding more time to the schedule to account for unknowns may give you a more accurate schedule, but it will also likely become a self-fulfilling prophecy.

The solution I recommend is to use two schedules: an aggressive one for the project team and a second schedule that's communicated outside to others that represents the most likely schedule, allowing for some typical delays in the development process.

In recent years it's become less clear just when a product is done. It's become possible to introduce a product and then continue to "finish it" after it's in the customer's hands. More and more products can be updated or have software-related bugs fixed by the customer by connecting the device to a computer and downloading new software. This is commonly done with cell phones, cameras, GPS devices, and even toys. It reduces the need for the product to be "feature complete" before being released.

Often delays occur because of the need to add more features. That's why the MRD was developed, so you can prioritize which features are really important. It may just be that a product will have fewer features than planned to stay on schedule, or be improved through software updates months later.

Apple cleverly took this to a new art form. When the iPhone was introduced, many features were missing, but over time many of them were added, along with genuinely new features through software upgrades. Customers were delighted to be able to get "new features at no added cost," when in fact the original product was not quite done when introduced. Of course, it depends on what the product is; Microsoft Windows Vista, which shipped with many deficiencies, created many dissatisfied users, even after the upgrades became available.

What's the best way to maintain and develop a schedule? While some use Microsoft Project, a powerful scheduling software program, for most products I have found this to be overkill. Too often it takes nearly a full-time effort to keep it up to date, and its value relies on providing more details than are usually available, such as a person's available time many months out. I prefer to prepare and manage a schedule using a spreadsheet with a list of key milestones, due dates, and responsibilities updated weekly. Every team member has the list and understands the milestones for which he or she is responsible. While Project shows dependencies of one activity on another, close collaboration of team members can be equally effective at understanding how one member's work affects the others.

Another danger using Project is that it identifies the activities on the critical path and provides slack or extra time to perform all the other (noncritical) activities. (The *critical path* is the series of activities that take the longest to complete, and therefore determines the completion date of a project.) If people whose tasks are not on the critical path take the full time available, then every task tends to move to the critical path, increasing the number of activities that can set back the schedule.

Rather than using dates determined by a schedule, practicality usually prevails, establishing due dates to be those of major trade shows, such as CES (a trade show sponsored by the Consumer Electronics Association), the National Hardware Show, CTIA (the trade show for the International Association for the Wireless Communications industry), and CeBIT (a major European computer, phone, and consumer electronics show). Because these dates are set in stone, they're excellent motivators for meeting an important target. I'm convinced one of the main benefits of these trade shows is to keep projects on schedule!

Finally, adding resources to stay on schedule and get to market sooner is often easy to justify by the added revenue from early sales. Adding two engineers for three months might cost $75,000. If that brings a $100 retail product selling 5,000 units per month to market one month sooner, that's additional revenue of $500,000, providing perhaps $200,000 in gross profit and $125,000 after paying for the cost of the added engineers.

Product Cost

The product cost has a big influence on the sales volume and the success of a product, yet is one of the areas that's often not considered until late in development.

Surprisingly, the errors come less from estimating the cost of the product and more from not carefully understanding the markups required to get the product from the factory to the marketplace. Nearly every inventor-engineer client I have worked with has failed to take into account and develop a detailed understanding of how the product's cost will translate into the retail cost, and when they learn, it often appalls them. It's not unusual for the retail price of the product to be 4 to 5 times that of the material cost of the product. The following analysis explains.

BREATHIN—AN EXTENDED EXAMPLE

Consider a typical electro-mechanical consumer product that has a circuit board, plastic enclosure, display, and some mechanical parts. This description fits hundreds of products being made today, as far ranging as cell phones, GPS devices, iPods, digital cameras, pocket TVs, and radios.

For this example I'll use "BreathIn," a (hypothetical) pocket breathalyzer illustrated in Figure 3.2 and being manufactured in China for the BreathIn company.

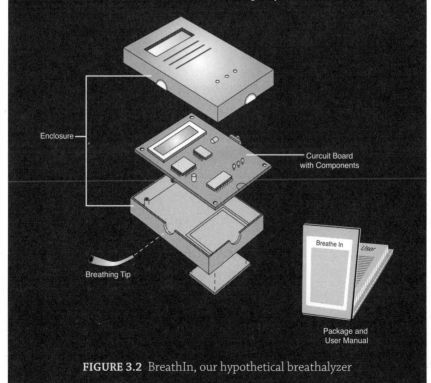

FIGURE 3.2 BreathIn, our hypothetical breathalyzer

The cost is calculated as follows:

Parts cost (called BOM costs, for Bill of Materials)
Enclosure, breathing tips $ 4
Circuit board with components $12
Packaging and user manual $ 2

BOM cost $18
Direct labor (DL) cost (the cost of putting the
product together) is 10% of the BOM $1.80

The sum of these costs equals the total direct cost (TDC):

TDC = BOM + DL
TDC = BOM + .10 BOM = 1.10 x BOM = $19.80

The factory cost (FC), what the manufacturer charges,
equals the total direct costs plus his indirect costs, namely
the manufacturing overhead, indirect labor, and profit.

Overhead and indirect labor include the factory's management and buyers' salaries, the inspectors, the building and
facilities. Profit is about 5% to 10%. All of this typically
totals about 30% of the TDC.

Thus, factory cost is

FC = TDC x 1.30 = (BOM x 1.10) x 1.30 = BOM x 1.43 =
$25.74

This says that the factory cost equals the BOM (material
costs) plus another 40% to 50%.

A good rule of thumb: The cost of a product is calculated by
adding up the parts costs (BOM) and multiplying by 1.5.
The 1.5 adds a little more than shown above to account for
shipping and amortization of the tooling. (Amortization is

the cost of tooling for the product that is paid off by adding a small amount to each product you sell.)

BreathIn Final Cost (BFC) = 1.5 x BOM cost

For this example, assume BFC = $27

But this cost has little resemblance to what customers will pay for the product. Their cost depends on the channels of distribution, or who "touches" the product between BreathIn and the customer. It varies widely, but usually there's plenty of precedent in each industry to figure it out. What's hard for some to accept is that often the retailer makes more money on the sale of each product than the company that developed it.

Assume the product is sold to a retail store such as Best Buy for SC (store cost).

The selling price BreathIn needs must provide it with enough margin to pay for the cost of the product, R&D, warranty, employees, and overhead, and still make a reasonable profit. Depending on its cost structure, that means BreathIn needs a 25% to 60% margin. Let's use 50%. (Chapter 8, "Distribution: Getting Your Product to the Customer," provides more details.)

SC = BFC/(1-.50) = 27.00/.50 = $54
Best Buy's cost is $54

Now Best Buy will mark the product up to their selling price (SP), which is the price their customer will pay. That varies by product category and the demand for the product.

Their margin may be as little as 10% to 15% for computers and flat-panel TVs to as high as 50% to 70% for computer and phone accessories, where

%Margin = 100 x (SP – SC)/SP

For example, a product retailing for $100 that costs Best Buy $70 has a 30% margin.

For our BreathIn product, let's assume a margin for Best Buy of 46% resulting in a selling price (SP) of $100.

So, recapping, the BreathIn product made with $18 worth of materials will retail for $100, more than 5 times the cost of the materials. The store gets $43 and BreathIn gets $27 (see Figure 3.3).

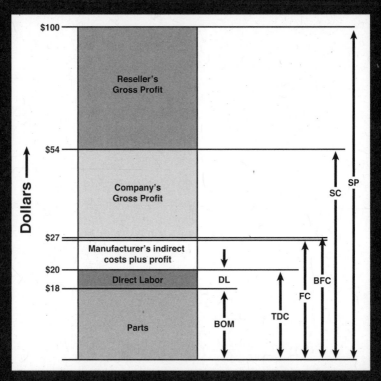

FIGURE 3.3 Product cost stackup

Every design decision you make will impact cost. If you've established a need to retail your product for $100 adding $1 in materials adds $5 to the retail. Likewise, lowering costs by reducing the number of parts through clever engineering has a 5 times multiplier. Engineers with experience in developing consumer electronic products are sensitive to combining multiple functions into a single part and look for savings of even a few cents from a variety of areas, as it all adds up.

While this discussion covers what goes into the product cost, the price of the product, what the customer is willing to pay, has no relation to its cost.

While you don't want to sell a product at a price that's below its cost, the customer will pay a price based on how desirable the product is, its uniqueness, the competition, and how else the problem can be solved.

I've intentionally grouped the development process with marketing and other non-engineering factors that, based on conventional thinking, may seem not to belong. But today it's a big mistake to develop a product without considering the who, what, when, and how much of the product.

CHAPTER 4

Industrial Design Matters

It need be no more expensive to build a product with good ID than bad.

While much of the product development process involves engineers developing mechanical, electronic, and software designs, there's one element that I've always considered to be one of the most important parts of creating a successful consumer technology product: industrial design.

Industrial design (ID) encompasses the appearance, aesthetics, and usability of a product. It's so powerful that it can impact the emotional bond between the product and the user. As products become smaller, more personal, and carried with us so much of the time, they become expressive of who we are. Thus, ID becomes even more important.

Usability, how the user interacts with the product, the software menus, and its behavior, has become equally important. It's sometimes done by industrial designers or by usability experts working with the designers.

A mobile phone is a good example where appearance and usability are far more important than what's inside. Motorola's handset business struggled for a number of reasons, but the lack of consistently good and imaginative industrial design and the poor usability of its software were major causes. In contrast, the Apple iPhone's attractive ID and simple user interface has set new standards and raised the bar for the industry. Although the Motorola Razr has a good ID, the company was unable to transform it into an "experience," as Apple does. Instead, they tried to milk the ID, creating numerous iterations of the one design.

While it's the engineer's role to develop a product that performs the specific functions accurately, efficiently, and reliably, it's the industrial designer's responsibility to design how the product looks, to determine how it relates to the user's senses, and to make it simple and delightful to use. Industrial designers often take responsibility for the relationship between the product and user, which heavily influences the development.

There are many ways for the engineering team to design and assemble a product's functional components: the circuit board, display, speaker, controls, and other parts. A product can be wide and flat or narrow and thick, and yet both containing the same components. The mechanical engineer can design an enclosure made from metal or plastic, painted or plated. Its edges can be softly rounded or sharply beveled.

For example, Sony and Apple each designed their 3-pound notebook computers differently (see Figure 4.1). Sony's ultra compact TZ model has a smaller footprint but is thicker than the Apple Air. As a result its keyboard is less than full size, the keys are closer together, and it has a smaller display. Apple chose a different approach, using a bigger display and a full-size keyboard, but made the MacBook Air so thin that they were not able to include an optical drive, a removable battery, and several connection ports.

That's where the industrial designers come in. They're trained to apply a sense of aesthetics and usability to products, making them appealing to look at and intuitive to use, while still meeting the functional requirements. Typically, industrial designers work with the design and marketing teams. But as in the previous example, two products starting with similar requirements, resulted in two very different outcomes.

FIGURE 4.1 Sony TZ and MacBook Air

The advancement of technology has given industrial designers even more opportunities to influence a design. New software used for designing the contours of a product's surfaces, and new machinery used to create the tooling to make the parts, allow the products to have unusually complex shapes and curves; they no longer need to be flat or cylindrical. The increasing use of displays adds new ways to interact with and to control the product.

With so much competition among so many products with similar functionality, the industrial design often makes the difference between a product's success and its failure. The overall appearance is the first thing the buyer sees, forming the initial impressions. The second thing a buyer notices is how easy or difficult it is to use or to communicate with the product. And customers are willing to pay more for products that excel in these areas.

Why are so many products today undistinguished looking and why do so few companies excel at doing good ID? Some companies don't want to take the time and spend the money to go through the process. And many products are designed and developed in Asia, isolated from the customer, and imported here without undergoing any changes.

Many companies have traditionally considered industrial design as an afterthought, a fine-tuning of the enclosure's shape, the placement of the buttons, or just the product's color. But that greatly diminishes the value of what good industrial design can be.

I've never been able to understand that attitude, other than attributing it to ignorance (or bad taste), because a product with good design need not cost more to manufacture than one with a poor design. Yet examples of products with mediocre designs are all around us. Most clock radios are ugly and difficult to use. Some are constructed out of plastic meant to look like wood, with garish red numbers, little buttons sprinkled on multiple surfaces, and printing too small to read, especially in dim light.

Bluetooth headsets are also notoriously ugly and hard to use, with their flashing lights and tiny buttons, each having a multitude of functions depending on the blinking pattern or how you push the buttons.

But some companies understand good design. Herman Miller's Aeron chair, which I've owned for ten years is a joy to use and to look at (see Figure 4.2). OXO, a housewares company, became known for its kitchen utensils with unusually comfortable and attractive handles, shown in Figure 4.3, and proving that good design need not be confined to expensive products.

FIGURE 4.2 Herman Miller Aeron chair

FIGURE 4.3 OXO Good Grips

Discovering ID

I discovered the value of industrial design in my first job as a design engineer at Polaroid. The company's industrial designer was Henry Dreyfuss, the founder of the modern industrial design movement. His company developed the ID for products such as AT&T telephones, Singer sewing machines, John Deere tractors, Hoover vacuum cleaners, and GE refrigerators, as well as most of Polaroid's products from 1963 to the 1990s.

I admired how Dreyfuss's designers were able to make a product come to life, giving it a unique personality and look. During the development of the SX-70 camera, Dreyfuss worked with Polaroid's Founder and CEO, Edwin Land to influence its shape, how it folded, and how it was held in the hand, as well as the innovative leather covering and brushed chrome finish.

On many of the products I developed, Dreyfuss was adept at turning a boxy design into something distinctive and memorable. The product often looked less intimidating and more inviting, yet still conveyed what it was supposed to do and how it worked.

In his book *Designing for People*, Dreyfuss describes how he first developed his skills. Macy's tried hiring him to improve the appearance and functionality of the products sold in their stores. They wanted him to recommend changes to the products' manufacturers. But Dreyfuss realized he could have a much bigger impact on the products by working for the manufacturers at the beginning of the design phase, because good design is built in, not added on as an afterthought.

By examining a company's products, it's easy to see what they value. Dell, for example, until recently hadn't placed much importance on industrial design. Their products have been boring, boxy, and utilitarian-looking; nothing distinguishes them from dozens of other commodity products from lesser-known companies.

Dell had been an operationally driven company where cost and simplicity were paramount. ID, which takes investment and adds cost that cannot always be measured, was difficult for the organization to accept. But as Dell began to suffer in the marketplace and as their customer base shifted more to consumers, selling more of their products through retail, they began to focus on improving ID. One of Dell's first new models during this shift was the XPS 1330, shown in Figure 4.4, which has garnered praise not only for its performance but also for its good looks.

FIGURE 4.4 A recent Dell notebook

Some companies don't emphasize industrial design because they think consumers don't care and are only interested in the lowest possible cost product. But I've always believed consumers are great judges of good industrial design and are usually out in front of the manufacturers. While customers may not be able to describe what they want, they buy well-designed products when they see them and use them more often. Good ID can provide the "wow" factor that can spark a customer's interest like few other things can.

Apple's products have tasteful designs and often utilize a common "design language" that people recognize even when no logo is visible. (*Design language* is a design term for the predetermined principles a designer uses to allow the product to communicate with a consumer. Many products have this conscious and well-thought-out aspect, whether it be Apple computers, OXO's Good Grip kitchen utensils, or BMW automobiles.)

Apple's designs use precisely fitting parts, smooth, optically polished white and black plastic, geometric shapes with rounded corners, simple controls, and matte finished aluminum enclosures. Every detail of the product is meticulously finished. The bottom of a Mac notebook is more attractive than the tops of many PC notebooks. Attention to detail extends to the packaging and how the products are placed within the package. I recently opened a product with several cables enclosed. Instead of the cable loops being tied using a twist tie, a clear plastic strip was used with an easy-to-grasp tab to quickly remove it. Customers notice this subtle message that says we respect your time and want to make it easy for you to set up your new product.

Over the years, Apple has created several different design languages. A decade ago they pioneered the use of translucent plastic in bubblegum colors of turquoise, orange, and green. Their next generation language moved to glossy white, and most recently they've created a language using elements of black and soft metallic finishes. The iPod family of products has been developed using several generations of design languages, yet can still be recognized by its iconic rectangles and circle, shown in Figure 4.5, giving it an advantage over its competition and building on its past success.

The Swiss Army pocket knife from Victorinox Swiss Army is another example of an instantly recognizable iconic product with its glossy red handle and gleaming stainless steel implements, branded with a silver cross on a red shield. It's so powerful that the company adapted some of these same design elements to create a successful line of watches and luggage.

The three-legged Weber kettle grill is a familiar backyard icon that's endured for more than fifty years. The popular apple-shaped kettle continues to be recognized as an image of simplicity and value, and is now available in a variety of sizes and models. It's even spawned a chain of restaurants based on the kettle grill icon.

Occasionally a product's industrial design can overtake function. Apple's MacBook Air, noted earlier, is an ultra-thin notebook with a stunning industrial design. Its aluminum enclosure provides the sturdiness needed for a portable product in one of the thinnest form factors ever. Yet a number of sacrifices were made that limit its functionality, particularly for those mobile business users who are on the road for long stretches of time. For example, while the thin and light design makes it perfect for travel, sealing the battery inside eliminates the option of carrying spare batteries to extend its run time beyond 3 hours. Apple's ads show the Air fitting into an envelope, yet I think Apple literally pushed the envelope too far. But because Apple has a good relationship with their customers, and is driven by design with a reputation for innovation, even when they miss the mark, people are more forgiving. Any other company that made these same compromises would likely be ridiculed.

When I developed the Seiko Smart Label Printer, I wanted to create something distinctive that bore no resemblance to common industrial label printers. David Lee, an industrial designer with Hauser Design, created an iconic design that combined two basic shapes, a cylinder and a triangular wedge, illustrated in Figure 4.5. The design was so successful that the same shape is being used in today's models, nearly two decades later. The ability of Seiko to retail the product for more than $200 at the time was as much related to its appearance as to its functionality.

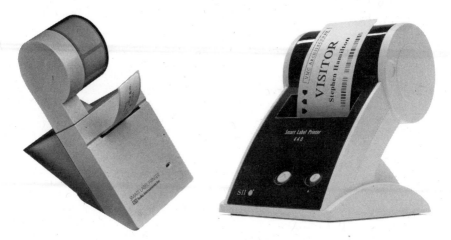

FIGURE 4.5 Seiko Smart Label Printer: 1990 and 2008

Conflicts between engineers and industrial designers are not uncommon. The engineers want to get the product finished, placing their emphasis on functionality rather than looks and not always recognizing the need for extra time and added complexity the industrial designer may ask for. The industrial designers at Apple were rarely deterred by engineers uttering the words "can't" or "this has never been done before."

Robert Brunner, the director of industrial design during my tenure at Apple, worked to reduce this natural conflict with engineers. He encouraged them to visit the industrial design department at any time to see what was going on. He understood the need for close cooperation between both groups, realizing that you can't get good ID without their support.

There's often a fine line between what is impossible and what is just difficult. Apple has always pushed their designs to the edge. They challenge their engineers to do things with materials and processes that have never been done before.

Shortly after the introduction of the iPhone I was reviewing a Nokia E61 smartphone for my technology column. At the time it was one of Nokia's top models, yet I saw many cosmetic defects I hadn't noticed before the iPhone. The metal housing showed deformities, and the fit between parts showed gaps. It looked crude by comparison to the iPhone.

That's a reflection of how Apple has raised the standards of acceptability, shown competitors what can be done, and taught manufacturers how to do it. That benefits the entire industry.

Companies need not go to the great lengths that Apple goes to if they don't have the resources or budget. There are plenty of opportunities to create a product with a very good industrial design that can set it apart from its competitors. Few companies have large industrial design groups, and it's often more practical to rely on outside design firms.

Selecting an industrial design company need not be a daunting process. It's a competitive industry with a number of excellent companies with capabilities in the consumer tech products area. In fact, a number of ex-Apple designers have started their own companies and provide equivalent capabilities.

Check out the winners of the annual design awards that appear in *Business Week* and *I.D.* (International Design) magazine each year as a start. Look for companies that design products for a similar audience. But don't stop there; dig deeper beyond the winning companies. Smaller companies or individual designers are often as good or better than big companies, but because they don't do as many projects they may not show up on these lists. Many of the large companies are also more expensive without providing any added benefits.

Recently I was hired by a Japanese computer peripherals company
to help them pick a US industrial design company to develop a new
design for one of their product lines. We identified a half dozen well-
recognized West Coast industrial design firms, provided the same
detailed request to each, and asked them to provide a proposal and
budget to accomplish the same tasks. They each were offered payment
for the work that went into their proposal.

The results were surprising. One of the largest, most well known of
the industrial design companies, submitted a proposal for $650,000,
that began with a study of the how the world perceives the product
category and included five more exploratory phases, before getting to
the design of the product itself.

A second company provided a more focused proposal for about
$300,000, and a third for $250,000. When the first company's estimate was challenged they quickly cut their price in half, which spoke
volumes about how much they believed in their original proposal. High
cost is one of the reasons I shy away from large firms and prefer working with smaller companies, where one of the principals will be doing
the design and will be more understanding of budget constraints.

I also look for companies that have experience in the same areas of
products and customers. Designing low volume medical devices is
different from designing high volume consumer products. While cost
is important, I place little value on the initial quotes, before digging
into the details. They often vary based on the designer's assumptions
about the extent of the project rather than differences between companies' hourly rates.

How much and what work a company performs depends on how well
you know your market, the competition, and the customer. If you
know very little or want a fresh look, then you can benefit by having

the ID firm do an exploratory phase; the results could provide an entirely new approach to the product.

Brunner, who now runs his own design firm, Ammunition, in San Francisco, designed a barbecue grill (the Fuego, shown in Figure 4.6) originally as an exercise for The Discovery Channel. He took an entirely fresh approach to a product staple that had changed little in decades. Most grills look much the same: a rectangular box with a hinged hood and controls along one edge. The biggest innovation in the past decade was changing the material on some models from cast iron and painted steel to stainless steel.

FIGURE 4.6 The Fuego grill

Before Brunner began his design, he studied how people interacted with a backyard barbecue grill. Most grills were used on a patio with the host barbecuing off in a corner isolated from his guests. Brunner considered a design without a hood, which acts as a barrier to socialization. Eliminating the hood would encourage the guests to gather around all four sides of the grill.

The Fuego's design evolved from this research about how the grill could best be used, rather than how grills were being used. The Fuego has been successful and sells at a premium price, in large part due to its unique design.

Another industrial designer, Gad Shaanan, was contracted by Hewlett-Packard to design a line of large screen TVs. You might think it would be difficult to come up with a design that could distinguish it from the scores of competitive models. But by watching how users set up their TVs, Shaanan developed a design in which the wires were routed from the back of the set around the side to a front compartment below the screen. A door folded down exposing all the connectors on the front of the set, making it a snap to set up.

The Industrial Design Process

1. **Your briefing**: The client briefs the designer, providing a description of the product and how it's intended to be used and provides supporting information such as the MRD, specification, competitive data, and other pertinent industry information.

2. **Initial design ideas**: The designer develops ideas and presents them using a number of rough sketches illustrating a design language and a variety of design ideas.

3. **Discussion and refinement**: The client and the designer review the ideas and sketches, and the client provides feedback. The designer often goes through one or two additional iterations.

4. **Final design**: The designer refines the designs to a few and builds nonworking models that simulate the product's appearance.

5. **Documentation**: After there's agreement on the final ID, it's developed into CAD drawings and electronic files that describe the materials, colors, and other details.

Because of the impact of Asia, the industrial design field is going through some major upheavals. Many companies that outsource their ID prefer a company that takes the product through the design and into the manufacturing stages, particularly now that more is being done in Asia. As a result, more industrial design firms are collaborating with Asian manufacturers to offer a single point of contact.

My advice is not to follow this model of utilizing one firm to do both the industrial design and the manufacturing. Using the one firm is often more costly, and it's likely the manufacturer that firm collaborates with will not be the most appropriate one for your particular product. Take responsibility for selecting and managing your own manufacturer. Find the best manufacturer you can and nurture that relationship directly. Likewise, find the best industrial designer for your product and don't be influenced by other factors.

How much should you pay for ID? It varies with the type and complexity of the product and how much needs to be done. For a product with the mechanical complexity of a GPS, an MP3 player, earphones, a phone, or a computer peripheral, you can find industrial designers who charge as little as $20,000 to as much as hundreds of thousands of dollars. If you have a reasonable budget, many will work within it and still provide good results. They just may reduce the number of alternative designs.

But don't skip it. A good industrial design will increase your chances for success. It adds another dimension to the product that says much about the kind of company you are and your appreciation for doing things that are out of the ordinary. Because so few companies even try, it's not difficult to stand apart from the crowd if you do it well.

CHAPTER 5

Why Outsource?

Shenzhen is the manufacturer to the world for consumer electronics.

You no longer need to be a Sony with your own design staff and factories to build world-class products. Where making sophisticated electronic consumer products once was the privileged domain of a few, now virtually anyone can play. The advantage is now to the swift and the creative, rather than the big. But to get that advantage you'll need to go to Asia.

The Rise of the OEM and ODM Model

Companies that produce products for customers who brand, distribute, and market them under their own names are called *original equipment manufacturers* (OEMs) and *original design manufacturers* (ODMs). OEMs are companies that manufacture the product while ODMs both design and manufacture them. Some OEMs and ODMs have grown so large and capable that it's even common for them to make products for customers who compete with one another.

One of the most successful examples has been the manufacturing of notebook computers in Taiwan. Inventec Electonics Corporation, for example, is one of the largest ODM notebook companies in the world and has been making products for Hewlett-Packard, Toshiba, and several others. Quanta, another huge ODM, makes notebooks for Apple, Dell, and Hewlett-Packard, as well as others. It's typical for the large computer companies to use several ODMs.

I used the ODM model when I worked for Apple. I selected Inventec to design and make the second-generation Newton, and Quanta to design and make the PowerBook 1400, the first Apple notebook to be both designed and built in Taiwan.

The leading notebook manufacturers, including Inventec and Quanta, have become so experienced at building the products that they've taken over much of the design from their customers. They have the relations with the component suppliers, are the first to learn of and incorporate new technologies, and have become skilled at rapidly creating new models. Not only do they make and manufacture the notebooks, some companies manage the delivery process as well, shipping the finished product directly to the end customer within a few days after the customer ordered it.

This model is now being replicated across many other categories of consumer electronic products and in other Asian countries, as well. Thousands of OEM and ODM companies specialize in manufacturing and designing specific types of products for their customers who, in turn, take them to market under their own brands. Where once a company that branded a product did almost everything from design to manufacturing, that's no longer the case.

From my experience in developing many products using OEMs and ODMs in Taiwan and China, Taiwan is exceptionally strong in its engineering and manufacturing skills, and China in its manufacturing, infrastructure, and cost advantage. Although China is not strong in the design of technically complex products, their skills are constantly improving.

Japan, where I began doing ODM products, has become too expensive, and no longer is competitive. And with their established worldwide brands, Japanese companies do less ODM work for others and focus on their own products.

Taiwan

Taiwan is home to some of the most technically proficient engineers who have expertise in designing and manufacturing complex consumer electronics products in high volume. Many Taiwanese companies offer engineering skills comparable to Japanese and Western companies, but with the entrepreneurial attitude of Silicon Valley engineers. They have a positive can-do attitude, are resourceful, and strive to meet their commitments.

Taiwan has grown rapidly in its ability to design sophisticated technology products. Taiwanese companies produce 90% of the world's notebooks. That, in turn, has propelled the growth of related industries, such as flat-panel displays, chips, modems, GPS technologies, as well as advanced materials used for notebook enclosures. In recent years, many Taiwanese companies have moved their factories to China for cost savings and to have access to more engineers, but these factories are still run and staffed by Taiwanese.

I recently worked with a Taiwanese company that designs and manufactures GPS devices to create a similar product for a client. Time to market was much faster and much less expensive than if my client tried doing it himself. The Taiwanese company has a team of skilled engineers who had the experience, proven designs, and relationships with all the necessary suppliers. This model is used day in and day out by numerous Western companies for developing a wide array of products.

Taiwan's transformation has been a stunning achievement. I first visited Taipei, Taiwan's capital, in 1983 when I was developing phones for Atari. My guide was a manager for a power supply company, Stan Glascow, who led the way over dirt roads to a factory making audio boom boxes. A lot has happened since. Stan is now president of Sony Electronics of America, and Taipei is a modern city with a new

subway system, highways, and tall skyscrapers. The road to the air-
port, once lined with military outposts, guarding against an invasion
from mainland China is now a superhighway.

Taiwan's living standards are now not much different from ours. As
a result it's losing the competitive manufacturing advantages it once
had. But it still remains the best place for finding entrepreneurial
companies and engineers for turning complex electronic product
ideas into successful products.

Taiwan also has a special link with the mainland. Although there continues to be political squabbling between the two, Taiwan's technology companies have made huge investments in the mainland. They've
built hundreds of modern factories, many in the Shanghai area, less
than 2 hours from Taipei by plane.

Because of Taiwan's entrepreneurial skills and experience working
with Americans and Europeans, there are few cultural problems.
Taiwanese companies generally are easy to work with. They require
little supervision, few visits, and they communicate clearly. Taiwanese
individuals who work with US and European customers even have
adopted Westernized first names.

The alternative to working with Taiwanese companies is working with
Chinese companies. This works best for less-complex products that
are more fully developed and closer to being production-ready. Chinese engineers and management are much less experienced than their
Taiwanese counterparts and require much closer supervision.

Mainland China

The Pearl River Delta area of the southern China province of Guangdong has grown over the past 25 years to become the manufacturing
center of the world. Well-known for manufacturing textiles, footwear,

leather goods, toys and appliances, Guangdong has become the center of manufacturing for consumer electronics, such as audio equipment, handheld electronics, cell phones, computers, cameras, MP3 players, printers, and much more. The growth has been fueled by investments in these factories from Hong Kong, Taiwan, the United States, and Europe. These factories now consume half the integrated circuits manufactured in China.

While much of this growth was the result of Western companies looking for lower manufacturing costs, that's no longer the primary reason for going to China. It's as much because of the huge infrastructure of manufacturers and suppliers concentrated around the city of Shenzhen at the mouth of the delta, just a 1-hour train ride from Hong Kong.

Walk through the factories and you'll see products from competitive companies being built on different floors. Everyone benefits from the economies of scale that these manufacturers are able to attain.

The infrastructure is made up of thousands of suppliers of electronics, displays, circuit boards, moldings, packaging, power supplies, and other components. These suppliers feed components and partial assemblies to the manufacturers, who then assemble, test, and ship the products. They try to do it on a "just in time" basis, reducing the need for stocking huge inventories, and, as a result, lowering costs and reducing the risk of obsolete products.

With suppliers all within an hour or two of one another, time to market has improved so that it's become faster to get a product built in Asia and delivered to a customer in the United States, Europe, or elsewhere than to do it all in the United States or Europe—if, in fact, that were even possible. And should you need to solve a problem, your suppliers can respond within hours, not days or weeks.

I worked with a Hong Kong company, SolarWide, to develop a digital tape measure for Seiko Instruments. Product was scheduled to be shipped on a Tuesday to Macy's, where it was to be featured in its Sunday ad supplement, which had already been distributed to newspapers across the country. Tuesday afternoon we discovered a problem that required a part to be changed. We contacted the supplier, who sent engineers to the plant within the hour to assess the situation. They then worked through the night to make the new parts, and delivered them on Wednesday at 7 a.m. The product was reworked and shipped that afternoon, still in time to reach the stores for the weekend sale. This was not the exception, but an example of the way things work there.

Asia's Advantage

Unfortunately, it's become difficult to build these products competitively in the United States or Western Europe, because many of the parts come from Asia. Furthermore, it's also becoming more difficult to design products in the West that are to be made in Asia. Domestic companies don't have the same access to many of the parts and road maps of future parts needed in new products. Component manufacturers set up their sales and support offices close to their customers, where the products are made. So, as manufacturing moved offshore, the expertise and support went, as well.

A client developing a handheld computer in the United States needed a 4-inch color display but was unable to learn much from the suppliers' distributors and reps in the United States. The client's engineers tried their best, selecting a screen available from the local distributor to build the product.

But when my client engaged an Asian manufacturer, the product needed to be redesigned for production. The display he had chosen was being discontinued, replaced by one with different dimensions.

Some of the electrical components selected by the engineers were more expensive than others available in China, and the circuit board needed to be redesigned to work on the manufacturing equipment in China. The US design had been done without knowledge of the Asian manufacturing requirements, adding months to the schedule and wasting money on a design that couldn't be used. Unfortunately, this occurs all too often.

Is Outsourcing for All?

Outsourcing in Asia is not for all companies and products. The technology products and scenarios best suited for manufacture in China are

❖ Small electronic devices containing circuit boards, displays, motors, plastic moldings, and sheet metal parts. Electronic components are readily available at some of the lowest pricing in the world, and millions of circuit boards are manufactured each day. The cost of plastic tooling and molding is usually less than half the cost in the United States or Western Europe, and it takes less time to build it.

❖ Production volumes should be thousands per month rather than hundreds. It makes little sense to go to China for products with low volumes of fewer than 1,000 items per month, particularly if the product cost is less than $50. Yearly business should be at least $200,000 to $300,000 in the first year and have a good chance of growing to at least a $500,000 or more a year or two later.

❖ The more mature a design the better. Products that are complex or still going through design changes are best built locally where the engineers can spend more time debugging the design. While engineers in China can work on production level problems, few are equipped to solve complex design issues. Today, China works best when most the serious design deficiencies have been eliminated. Taiwan is different, and I would not hesitate to have a product designed from the ground up there.

❖ You need to be adequately funded. You'll be making substantial investments in inventory and tooling that require prompt payment. Some of the manufacturers require companies whose products they take on to be backed by venture capitalists or major corporations. Because they work on small margins, credit is rarely provided.

❖ The product should be of high value and of relatively small dimensions so shipping costs will not be a burden. That makes consumer electronics ideal.

❖ Have a sound business plan. Your product should have good distribution and the potential for selling in reasonable quantities, as noted previously. One of the first questions you will be asked is how you plan to get your product to market. While few ask for guaranteed minimum quantities, they need to believe in the product's potential as well in the company's business model. Companies in Asia are cognisant of our consumer channels, retailers, and business activities, thanks to the Internet and experience with other customers.

❖ Any company that goes to China should have sufficient resources in time, manpower, and money for managing their activities there, including having people frequently on-site.

Low volume products, such as medical devices, in which there is less price pressure, are best done locally; the overhead costs, primarily the cost of travel and personnel spending time in China, can be significant. Still, many low volume products can benefit by building the tooling and parts in Taiwan or China, where costs can be one-third to one-half of those in the United States or Europe.

Going to China is not a solution in itself. It's an option that can be beneficial if done correctly; so set your expectations appropriately. No company is going to be so good that you'll be able to drop off your idea and pick up a finished product six months later. Instead, expect to be working far away from home for long periods of time to nurture your product along.

Chinese companies are not monolithic, just as Western companies are not all the same. There's a huge range of competency in China from companies with a few salespeople to those with broad capabilities. The challenge is finding the good ones.

Protection of Your Intellectual Property

One of the most frequently asked questions I get is whether a product brought to China to be manufactured will be copied. After all, China has a reputation for copying everything from designer purses to expensive watches to software. Do you face a risk of using a company to build your product if it's already making a product like yours? Will they copy your ideas and incorporate them into their own products or, worse, into your competitors' products?

I have never once encountered an overt act of a manufacturer copying products that were then sold to others. Never. Perhaps I've been lucky to work with companies that don't engage in these practices. Certainly it happens to some. But the overt copying is done mostly by different types of companies, not OEM and ODM companies whose business model depends on trusted relations with their customers, on whom they depend for most of their business.

Still, there are some ways to protect a design if you're concerned. Consign a unique part or custom chip to your manufacturer, but produce it elsewhere. Or manufacture parts of your product in several different factories and bring them to another company to do the final assembly.

But do note that a manufacturer may gain new skills just by building products for their customers. They become aware of new designs and new markets, and of course how well the products sell. From my experience, the advantages of working with a company with experience making similar products, vastly outweigh trying to work with a company without that experience. But remember that once a product goes on sale and is on the market, the design is readily available to be reverse-engineered and copied by anyone.

Ultimately, the best antidote to your product being copied is speeding your time to market, expanding distribution quickly, and working on your next generation product while your competitors are busy copying your old one. The best lawyers and the best patents won't help in the short term, and often are of little value in the long term, particularly with product lives being shorter than ever. Put your money in product development and marketing rather than in lawyers.

I do recommend signing an NDA (nondisclosure agreement) and developing a simple agreement or letter of intent, but I've rarely waited for an agreement to be completed before beginning the project. Delays in the early part of the project can never be made up. I've begun many projects on a handshake and have never regretted it. I discuss this in more detail in Chapter 9, "Legal Advice: Knowing When to Ignore It."

Product Quality

China is often in the news for producing products of poor quality. A number of consumer product companies have had to recall their products, everything from dog food to medication to toys, primarily because the products contained dangerous substances or ingredients.

If you believe the comments of politicians and talk show "experts" you'd think that China is the last place you'd want to make products. From my own experience these comments are misinformed and fail to address the real causes.

China has the broadest and most comprehensive manufacturing infrastructure in the world. Generalizing that products from China are good or bad, safe or dangerous means nothing. While China deserves some of the blame for failing to police its own industries, with its huge growth, this would be hard to do anywhere.

Nearly every product being sold in the United States or Europe that comes from China has a local company behind it. These companies are producing or procuring a product there and then importing it and distributing it under their own name. A company's role and responsibility, wherever they produce a product, and particularly when they sell it under their own brand name, is to oversee the development and manufacturing and ensure the product meets the requirements through careful inspection and auditing of production.

The companies with the tainted products failed to do this. They allowed defective products to reach the market because they didn't adequately oversee their manufacturing and then failed to perform inspection and testing that would have caught the defects. When a consumer buys a product, he expects the company whose brand is on that product to take responsibility for it.

Many Chinese manufacturers, particularly of nontechnical products, are not sophisticated. They're trying to produce products at low cost to please their customers and to make a profit. They're constantly using a network of suppliers, some of whom use their own suppliers. At each step along the way there's the incentive to cut costs to generate a little more profit.

Once production begins, some manufacturers or their suppliers may substitute lower cost materials or finishes. Some of these shortcuts are a result of carelessness or greed, or a result of the constant pressure to cut costs from the customer. Employees in these companies might not even understand how the cost cutting impacts and compromises the product because they are so far down the chain. That's why the company whose brand goes on the product needs to monitor the chain of manufacturers and constantly audit the product.

When under pressure to lower costs, the manufacturer's pricing may seem to be the first place to push. But putting pressure to cut costs can be harmful in the long run. I found this out the hard way.

When Palm requested a drastic cut in the cost of the folding keyboard that we were supplying, we, in turn, put pressure on Pertech, our supplier. Pertech made some concessions, but would not reduce the cost to us enough to meet Palm's demands. We found another supplier who quoted a 30% lower cost. But it turned out to be a costly mistake. The new supplier took almost a year to get into production due to quality problems and the inability to find competent suppliers.

The Chinese Factory

I've visited dozens of factories in China. Most are unpretentious buildings that have assembly lines in large open areas. Buildings are usually two to five stories in height with the factory floor on several of the upper levels. The lower levels typically house a shipping area and docks, warehousing, and inspection areas along with office personnel.

The buildings often look older than they really are, because of their constant around-the-clock use and stark, no-frills construction (see Figure 5.1). Rarely do you see automated equipment, other than in those factories that build printed circuit board assembles or make plastic parts. Most products are assembled by hand by young women in their late teens and twenties.

FIGURE 5.1 A Chinese factory

Working conditions of consumer product manufacturers are generally adequate, but with few frills. I have rarely encountered a factory with the poor working conditions so frequently described in the media. While factories with poor conditions certainly do exist, they are more commonly those making low-end nontechnical products.

Long tables with conveyer belts are set up in the open areas with the assembly operators sitting along one side (see Figure 5.2). Partially assembled products move from worker to worker, as each adds another part or performs a test. Instruction sheets hang above each operator's position, describing the job she performs.

Factories use workers rather than machines to put together the products because that provides the flexibility to quickly change what's being made. An assembly line can be quickly reconfigured to make another product.

FIGURE 5.2 A Chinese factory (inside)

This certainly runs counter to the predictions made through the years that factories of the future would be populated by fewer workers and, instead, by automatic machinery and robots. While such equipment is used for some products that have long lives and high value, such as notebooks and printed circuit boards, it is impractical for building products that have short lives and change so quickly. (Some notebook factories are in a class by themselves: modern, air-conditioned work areas, plus cafeterias, gymnasiums, modern dorms, and even movie theaters and libraries.)

After a product is built and tested, it's packaged at the end of the line and then goes to the shipping area for transport to the customer. Before shipping an inspector will pick out sample units to test. And products that have complex electronics are often turned on and run for a day to ensure there are no early failures.

Watching your product roll down the assembly line, being built by the thousands, is one of the most satisfying moments during the development of a product. It's a sight that sometimes you think will never arrive. You've gone from struggling for months to get one unit to work, to seeing thousands being built, all working perfectly. That's the moment you go from worrying about making it to worrying about selling it.

CHAPTER 6

Selecting and Working with an Asian Partner

The skill levels of the Chinese workers are some of the best in the world.
—Steve Leveen, Levenger CEO

Assuming you meet the requirements of going to Asia discussed in Chapter 5, "Why Outsource?," one of the first decisions to make in selecting a company is to determine what kind of help you need. The most typical need, and one that can justify going halfway around the world, is to tap into the expertise of a manufacturer that builds products like yours. That provides a whole series of advantages:

❖ Faster time to market

❖ The knowledge and equipment to build and test products like yours

❖ Established relationships with and support from suppliers of components that will be used in your product

❖ Skilled engineers to support the development, production, and quality issues that inevitably surface

❖ Lower manufacturing cost

Therefore, select a company that already does or comes closest to doing what you need done. Find one with similar types of customers making similar kinds of products in similar volumes. You don't want a company so big that your business will be unimportant to them, nor so small that they don't have adequate resources to support your growth.

There's also less risk since they've already made the mistakes and have likely learned from them. In addition, the company has the testing and manufacturing equipment in place, which might otherwise cost you tens of thousands of dollars. They have the relationships with the suppliers and can buy parts at huge discounts, because they will be used not only on your products but also on similar products for others.

Think Outside took the product concept for building the Stowaway folding keyboard to Pertech, a small keyboard company in Taiwan. George Kao, the founder, had tremendous expertise and many years of experience in designing and building keyboards for notebook computers. The company had all the equipment in place for making the parts, printing the keys, assembling, and testing. Pertech's experience played a major part in our ability to solve technical problems and bring the product to market quickly.

Another factor in evaluating a supplier is its ownership. I've had much better experiences working with Taiwanese-owned companies in China. They have a stronger technology foundation, and the management usually resides on location in China. Many Hong Kong-owned companies rely on management that lives in Hong Kong and commutes to their factories, on-site for only three or four days a week. Chinese-owned companies often have a weaker management structure due to the difficulty of finding and retaining experienced Chinese managers and engineers.

Once you've identified prospective companies, contact them by e-mail explaining the type of product, the prospective volume, and what you are looking for. Indicate the state of completion of the design, and make it clear what your needs are. English is usually well understood by companies working with Western companies.

Make use of the Internet. The Web sites www.alibaba.com, www.globalsources.com, and www.hktdc.com list thousands of manufacturing companies that offer products for sale. However, many of them are trading companies or wholesalers and not the actual manufacturer. You'll often need to dig deeper. Unfortunately, many of the major manufacturers are not listed on these sites.

Visit trade shows, particularly those in Asia that specialize in your area of business; for example, the Hong Kong Consumer Electronics Show in October and Taiwan's Computex in June. One of the main purposes of these shows is for local companies to show their products and to look for OEM and ODM customers.

Another excellent source for identifying key manufacturers is iSuppli (http://www.isuppli.com). This US company analyzes technology products and publishes comprehensive reports, including teardowns of consumer electronic products with costs and bills of materials. They also can identify the leading OEM and ODM manufacturers and their customers.

Study a company's products; they are its DNA. Buy samples and take them apart. Look at the quality of construction, the circuit board, and the components. This tells you more about a company than anything else. But be sure that the company actually manufactures the product and doesn't subcontract it to another company. When you arrive for a visit, insist on seeing the product being made.

Ultimately, an arrangement needs to be based on a personal relationship, and it's best to see for yourself what the company's skills really are. If you're unsure of how best to assess the company, take along someone who specializes in Asia sourcing.

Beware of companies that build specific types of product, but do not have all the skills you require. Before selecting a company to build a GPS device in Taiwan, I visited two Chinese companies, each with a strong product line, a comprehensive Web site, and even with GPS in their companies' names! However, upon visiting, I discovered that both companies were just assembling parts designed and sourced elsewhere and both exhibited little knowledge of their products' designs. At one company, when I asked where the engineering department was, they pointed to one young man in a cubicle. While nearly all companies outsource some of their work, you want a company that has most of the core competencies you need in-house.

Don't expect to get something for nothing. Some companies searching for a manufacturer think they can offer their product for distribution in China in exchange for free tooling or other concessions. But that rarely works since your manufacturer probably knows less than you do about marketing in China. Don't nickel and dime, because it signals you may be a problem down the road.

Avoid using agents or middlemen who often represent one or more companies and take a commission on your product. That can be costly and often becomes a communications barrier between you and the supplier. You need to have a strong direct link for the relationship to work.

Once you've identified a number of potential companies, begin your due diligence by using the following example as a guide:

The product, a handheld device about the size of a flashlight, was designed to create a high velocity stream of air from its nozzle for use as a substitute for compressed air in a can. Its components included rechargeable batteries, an electronic circuit, motor, impeller, and an enclosure made of plastic and matte finished aluminum. The client wanted it to have the look and finish of an Apple product.

I began my search by identifying a dozen companies that made products using similar components, such as power tools, electric toothbrushes, and accessories for iPods. I included the third because they had experience using aluminum and plastic parts that met Apple's standards. I contacted each company by e-mail with a short introduction and a brief but vague description of the product, the approximate yearly volume, and a rough schedule. I also provided a description of the company it was for, including its name (which was a well-known brand). I then waited for their responses. Of the 12 inquiries, I received responses from six companies within five days, several within 24 hours. A seventh company responded in ten days, while the rest never answered.

I then sent each of the seven a detailed questionnaire relating to their products, capabilities, and company. The detailed questionnaire had several purposes: to find the best manufacturer for the product based on their expertise with similar products, their interest in the project, and how well matched they were for the size of this order. I asked questions about their products, engineering capabilities, organization, in-house skills, a list of customers, and whether they did similar work for others. Two were eliminated in this process that took another ten days, leaving five companies of interest.

I then asked each of them to sign a nondisclosure agreement (NDA) and then sent sketches of the product to prepare them for a visit. The design package I sent contained some dimensional sketches, typical of what's supplied by an industrial designer, but didn't identify the product's purpose, nor were the drawings detailed enough that they could be used to make a product.

The cost of the product was intentionally not discussed because none of the companies had enough information to provide accurate quotes, and raising that issue now would be a diversion. I would be requiring the selected company to provide an open bill of materials showing all costs.

I've also found that cost has rarely been the primary issue in selecting a manufacturer at the outset. Costs from companies in the same geographic area rarely vary by more than 10% when they use an open bill of materials. That's because the component costs, which are about 70% to 80% of the final cost, are similar among companies. Also, rarely is the design complete when your selection is made, and costs will change as the design progresses. By agreeing to a price based on a formula tied to the BOM cost at the inception means there's no pressure to finalize a cost before starting and no need to negotiate each time a design change occurs.

One of the most important steps in the selection process is visiting the companies to see the facilities in person and meet the engineers and management. I'm always amazed by what I can learn in these visits, both good and bad. It's the flat world's version of MBWA, the famous principle made popular by *In Search of Excellence*, "managing by walking around." I've seen everything from assembly lines where each activity is carefully controlled to others with assemblers talking on their cell phones while working. I've seen managers who are highly experienced engineers and others who are salesmen telling you what they think you want to hear. Had I not paid a visit to the GPS factory, I never would have known what their limitations were.

Finally, you'll want to obtain references from the companies. Talk to customers; find out their specific experiences, what worked well and what didn't. Was the company on time? How was the quality?

I wish I could tell you that following this process guarantees success. In spite of all the screening, reference checking, and visits, using a Chinese manufacturer is far from risk-free. It's not uncommon to find that well-intentioned companies miss schedules, produce poor quality products, change parts and processes on their own, and fail to communicate internally and with their suppliers.

In fact, I often commiserate with others developing products in China, comparing our experiences with different companies and sometimes wondering why we are there. The fact is, in spite of all the problems, there are few other places to go to get the job done.

Managing the Relationship

It's important to closely manage the relationship using your own employees or consultants to work closely with the manufacturer. This individual should have the project management skills needed to drive the development activities and schedule and to provide frequent and clear communications among all the team members and the Asian manufacturer. That means frequent visits to Asia as often as every four to six weeks. Trying to do it from afar, known as "keyhole management," rarely works. Each customer is competing for resources from your manufacturer, and it's all but impossible to succeed without frequent visits.

Manufacturing Costs

Once you engage a manufacturer you will be making substantial investments as you move toward production. Here's what to expect.

Tooling—Tooling to make plastic and other parts represents one of the costliest expenses and has the biggest impact on the schedule, usually taking about three to four months to build.

Cost varies widely depending on the complexity of the product, the number of parts, and its volume, but is generally in the five- or six-figure range. It's typically paid 50% at inception and 50% when production quality parts can be produced. Be sure you retain owner-ship of the tooling. You've paid for it and want the option of moving it to another company if you change manufacturers.

Production design—This involves taking your design and having the manufacturer complete it so that it can be more easily manufac-tured. Most companies will charge at their cost, and some may split or absorb the cost altogether as an enticement for your business. If you are going to be charged and you want to reduce your cash flow, many manufacturers will negotiate an arrangement where some or all of the cost is spread across a number of units by adding a small amount to the product cost. Typically costs for a project can run from $20,000 to $100,000 or more depending on the amount of work required.

Assembly fixtures—These are fixtures used to assemble the product that are specific to your product. The fixtures can vary from devices that position parts being assembled to special trays to hold the parts while they are being painted. Depending on the production volume, it can vary widely, from hundreds of dollars to tens of thousands of dollars.

Test equipment—This is equipment to measure, adjust, and test your product during and after assembly. An example is equipment that opens and closes the lid of a notebook computer to ensure it meets the durability requirements, or computers that are used to monitor your product's performance or make a setting.

Prototypes—Before shipping your product you'll build sample units at several stages during development to verify the engineering design, test the product using parts from the tooling, and then perform preproduction testing of products made on the assembly line. Volume can vary from several dozen to several hundred units at each of these stages, depending on your needs. The cost is usually 2 to 10 times the price you'll be buying the production product for. This is an area of cost that's often overlooked and can be substantial, running into the hundreds of thousands of dollars.

Long lead parts—Many manufacturers will ask you to pay in advance for parts that need to be ordered several months in advance to have them on hand when production begins. The cost can be in tens or even hundreds of thousands of dollars, depending on the parts and your volume.

Manufacturing Quality

One of the greatest concerns with a new product is that it works as expected and has few failures once it reaches the customer. That's a function of the design, the parts, and the manufacturing. A good design is easy to assemble and less dependent on the individual doing the assembly. Parts that snap together precisely are much better than parts that are glued together, since how they are positioned and the amount of glue used can easily vary among operators.

The quality of the components can also affect the product, and it's the manufacturer's responsibility to inspect the parts when they arrive at the factory. Finally, the manufacturing needs to be done accurately, following procedures that have been tested and proven to work.

A high volume product should not have more than a percent or two of defects that affect performance, called *functional defects*. It may have another percent or two of cosmetic defects, or appearance-related items. However, it's not uncommon for complex products to have much higher levels of defects early in their production. For example, some notebook computers have 10% to 15% functional defects in the first year. Some customer surveys have shown that iPods with hard drives had a 7% rate of defects in the first year.

In the early stages of production, quality testing and inspection should be done at the factory under the supervision of the customer's engineers. This is the first time large volumes are being produced by new operators, and it's not uncommon for problems to be discovered.

Normally, the customer will develop the tests and procedures to be done, and the limits of acceptability. Once production ramps up, and the initial problems are addressed, it's not practical for every unit to be inspected, so, instead, they are "sampled." Sampling means that a small number of units are randomly selected from a larger group, called a *lot*. Based on the number of defects in this small sample, it's possible, using statistical science, to make a reasonably accurate judgment about the entire lot, and either accept or reject it in its entirety. Units in lots that are rejected are then individually inspected, repaired if needed, and sampled again.

Durability Testing

Your product also needs to pass several other tests, which represent extremes of temperature, humidity, and handling. While the requirements vary by product, typical tests include subjecting the product to temperatures of 160° F, –20° F, and 120° F/90% humidity for hours at a time. In addition, a thermal shock test subjects the product to alternately high and low temperatures. Finally, the product is subjected to vibrations over a wide range of frequencies and a shock and drop test, both in its packaging and by itself.

These tests are designed to ensure the product continues to function even after being exposed to extreme conditions that may occur in normal use. I've found these tests to reveal many problems with the design and manufacturing, such as cracking of the plastic, screws falling out, and parts coming loose.

Consumer electronics products ideally should survive a drop of 36 inches to 48 inches on a linoleum-tiled floor. The product is typically tested by dropping it on all six faces and on its corners.

All electrical products that generate a frequency of 500KHz or higher, essentially most products with a microprocessor, require FCC testing to ensure their interference with other devices does not exceed a certain level. The manufacturer can do some testing, while other tests need to be done by an FCC-approved lab. Most municipalities and states also require electrical safety testing. It can be done by UL or ETL (Electrical Testing Labs). The approval time varies depending on the type of product and whether criteria exist for the product's category, but it's typically two to three months.

A CE (European conformity) mark means that the manufacturer declares that the product meets the European requirements for the particular product type. Depending on the requirements, tests are done by the manufacturer or by a recognized laboratory. Finally the RoHS (Restriction of Hazardous Substances) mark ensures that the product does not contain specific levels of hazardous materials. It originated in Europe, but is now becoming a requirement in other parts of the world, including the United States.

Cost of all these tests can range from $20,000 to $50,000.

CHAPTER 7

The Marketing Component

The foundation of good marketing begins with respect for the customer.

The role of marketing is to help make a product succeed in the marketplace and realize its sale potential by using a variety of activities. These include influencing the product's design, positioning the product and company to the outside, conducting market research, promoting the product using public relations and advertising, and understanding and communicating with the customers.

A marketing plan revolves around the relationship between the company and the customer. I've found that the foundation of a good program consistently begins with an attitude that shows respect for that customer.

Having respect affects the product and the way the company does business. It means providing a product that customers want (whether they know it or not), one that has a great industrial design that appeals to their aesthetic senses. The product performs well and does what it promises and does it without effort; it's a delight to use that often offers more than is expected.

Good marketing is the antithesis of the infomercials on late night TV that try to convince viewers to send in their money on a one-time occurrence for something that's overhyped and usually fails to meet expectations.

An excellent marketing program continues after the sale to provide unexpectedly good customer service that goes on to build a long and positive relationship with the customer. Let's examine some of these activities in more detail.

Product Definition

In the early stages of development, one of the most important efforts is defining what the product does, as well as what it doesn't do. In other words balancing the trade-offs. Complicating this is the dimension of time. You're defining the product a year or more in advance, trying to accurately estimate market needs and competition. This is articulated, in part, by developing the market requirements document (MRD) described in Chapter 3, "The Basics of Development." More importantly, it's where the foresight and vision of the product advocate or leader comes in, figuring out what customers will want far into the future, and where the enabling technologies will be at that time.

The developers of the iPod recognized the future availability of tiny low-cost hard drives combined with the advantages of digitized music. Developers of digital picture frames saw the falling costs of LCD displays as finally making them practical.

In the case of our Stowaway keyboard, we realized that personal computing devices were getting smaller and more powerful, yet our fingers remained the same size. We envisioned the need for a way to enter text into these devices that was easy to use yet something that could be as small as the tiny computers themselves. While other companies recognized the same need, their solutions of using undersized keys and keyboards that were projected onto a table were not practical. In short, it is not enough to recognize trends; you need to have a successful solution.

Market Testing

During the development of a product it's beneficial to get input from potential customers, particularly if the product is unique or if design trade-offs need to be made. Most products are a delicate balance between function and cost.

While those closest to the product know it best, sometimes they can be too close and too wedded to the design to see things objectively. Although you need not take outsiders' advice, you may find that a fresh look is valuable in shaping the final design. There are a number of ways to gather this marketing input. Focus groups, used extensively among large companies, are rarely one of those best ways, however.

Focus Groups

A focus group is a marketing exercise in which perhaps a dozen people sit in a conference room with a trained moderator to explore product ideas with them. The moderator's role is to ask questions and solicit answers. The goal is to figure out what the participants think, usually as a whole, and draw conclusions that help the product company design or modify its products. The information they gather is a collection of opinions rather than statistically valid conclusions.

Focus groups are used for everything from determining the color of a product, the design of its packaging, an acceptable cost, or whether a product is even a good idea. Several focus group sessions are often held in multiple cities across the country to provide demographics representative of the public at large.

Based on my experience, relying on focus groups to create a new product rarely works. It's highly unlikely that a group of people working in this environment are able to develop a product that's highly innovative. These products more often come from individuals who can think imaginatively and have strong knowledge of their customers and the competition.

Some of the most successful products defy conventional wisdom. Kodak dismissed the idea of an instant film camera when Dr. Edwin Land presented it to them. If Steve Jobs had relied on focus groups to develop the iPhone it would have turned out with dozens of buttons and a smaller screen.

Some of the best products are driven by those with a unique idea that don't let conventional wisdom get in the way. They often have the ability to understand what their customers want well before the customers knew they needed it.

Of course, they're not always right. Land's instant movies were a huge flop as was Jobs' Next computer. But it's doubtful that focus groups would have prevented either. They flopped more as a result of changing markets or weakness in the products' performances.

Today the best use of focus groups for new product development is to learn their likes and dislikes about competitive products and to make comparisons between your product options. A camera company might benefit by asking consumers to rate the appearance, size, or usability of similar models from their competitors in comparison with their own, or to select the finish on a new product. But focus groups can be costly; a single session might cost $10,000 or more. A good product manager or marketing manager with an understanding of how the products are used and familiarity with the competition can often do just as well for a lot less money.

Industry Experts

Sometimes it is important that you test your product assumptions and get feedback during the early stages of development, when key decisions are being made, and when making the wrong decision can doom or delay the product. The best way I've found to get this input is to conduct personal interviews with prospective customers, industry analysts, and product reviewers who cover and know the category. Polaroid provided products to well-known photographers such as Yosef Karsh and Ansel Adams (see Figure 7.1). They also sent employees to spend a week or two with them to better understand how the products were used. I was lucky enough to be one of those employees, and that experience changed the way I thought about products I went on to develop.

FIGURE 7.1 Yosef Karsh and Ansel Adams at a workshop for Polaroid employees in Yosemite

Every industry has consultants who are usually accessible to discuss your product and often can provide valuable insight. While they charge substantial fees to their large customers, they're often accessible to smaller companies and often will provide advice at little or no cost if it's an area of interest. At Think Outside, we worked closely with Tim Bajarin, a highly regarded consultant in the mobile computing area.

We also asked expert typists, some holding world records for speed typing, to try the keyboard and comment on its type-ability and key placement. The results confirmed that our product was comparable in performance to the best full-size notebook keyboards. But when we asked potential users to try opening and closing the device, some had difficulty finding where to push and pull. As a result we added color to make the closing tabs more visible.

Some product reviewers will be willing to look at a product or discuss details informally. Reviewers and technology columnists see and use more products than most any group, and can offer valuable advice. They're less likely to be enamored and impressed with claims, often have strong opinions, and most are willing to maintain confidentiality. As a reviewer I've looked at many products, and I sometimes wondered what the company was thinking. It's not difficult to judge a product's likelihood of success or identify particular issues that need to be changed based on what came before. As a designer I've shown concepts to reviewers for their opinions. I'd much rather hear their complaints in person than read them in a national newspaper.

Accept the feedback as just an opinion, but carefully analyze the response, particularly if you hear the same issue from several people. While Logitech, one of the largest marketers of desktop keyboards and mice, dismissed our keyboard as too expensive and not of interest to them, the idea was seen as having strong merit. Use these interviews to check your assumptions, determine which features are most useful, test what customers are willing to pay, and determine trade-offs.

The chance that these discussions will result in a leak to a competitor or to the public is slim. Getting the feedback is more important. Most products fail because they're not bought, not because word gets out too soon.

Other Methods

Once a product is released, early market feedback is extremely valuable. While you think you know a product that you've sweated over for months, you really know it only after many units get into the hands of customers. Things you worried about may not be an issue, while other items you've dismissed or ignored can surface as problems.

When the second generation of Newton was launched we were interested in obtaining immediate feedback. So I sent part of the team to Apple's call center in Austin to both listen in on the first calls coming in from the early customers and take some of the calls themselves. Of course, now it can be done remotely, but this early feedback provided information well before the official reviews were in. We found that our concern about battery life was not an issue, but the newly developed soft-touch paint on some early products showed early wear, causing us to make immediate production changes. And of course we got an earful about its handwriting recognition.

Today some of the earliest feedback comes from the Internet. Many companies have user discussion boards where customers can post questions or comments. Apple's discussion site is a good source for gaining early product information on its products. It contains both the good and the bad customer experiences without any censorship.

Amazon offers a huge bonanza of valuable feedback on products it sells. Most are intelligent comments with a lot of detail and useful information. It's a great way to learn about the competition as well. However, still be cautious. When Amazon's Kindle electronic book reader was announced, there were several hundred vociferous opinions on the product—before it had even been shipped!

Once there's an established customer base that you're able to reach by e-mail, online surveys can provide a big help in getting feedback. The response rate is usually many times higher than other methods. Companies such as SurveyMonkey, QuestionPro, and others provide the online tools to easily set up and conduct them.

Product Positioning

When your product is introduced to the market you need to describe it, or position it, in a way that's accurate, clear, concise, and makes one want to buy it. Many companies make the mistake of providing a description with too much information. In these times, where we're being bombarded with all sorts of complicated messages from all directions, less is better.

Start with the product positioning statement for internal use that's a description of the product, its benefits, what is different from the competition and how you want the customer to perceive it. Then create a short statement for public consumption that supports this.

A client created an earphone that works like an earplug to seal out surrounding noise. It also reproduces sound more accurately than any of its competition. The positioning was "Exceptional sound isolation and highly accurate music reproduction." In eight words they were able to convey what the product does and its benefits. Think Outside's keyboard was positioned as the first full-size keyboard that fits in your pocket. Both are simple, understandable, accurate, and with no exaggeration.

The clever new Flip Video, a $150 video camera that takes video more easily than any other product, has become a huge hit. Its message is "Shoot anything, share everything"—quite an improvement from the typical, spec-laden messages of conventional video cameras (see Figure 2.3).

As a reviewer I receive scores of press releases and announcements of new products each week. If I can't understand what the product is, what it does, and who wants it, within 30 seconds, I move on. I've found that the longer the explanation, the less useful the product.

Creating the message is even more important with technology products loaded with features. A recent product I worked on was a pocket-sized device that has cellular data connectivity, live TV, a GPS, a music player, a camera, a picture viewer, and an Internet browser. We described it as "A pocket device with mobile TV and precise navigation," focusing on two of its strongest features.

Failure to position your product the way you'd like it to be viewed in the marketplace means that others will instead. First impressions can be difficult to change. The Apple Newton MessagePad was positioned as the first device that would recognize handwriting. Much of Apple's messaging for a year prior to the introduction kept reinforcing this. It set expectations that could never be met.

Unfortunately, no one with full knowledge of the product had carefully thought through this positioning. Would it work with all types of handwriting? Only printed words? How could it read handwriting that we can't even read? Apple's engineers really believed their handwriting technology would work, but they naively failed to realize the complexity of the problem for certain situations. Marketing wanted to highlight the product's uniqueness and built their PR on this unique attribute that they heard about from the engineers. When the product was introduced it could never meet the high expectations set for it; it became the butt of jokes and never recovered.

If the Newton MessagePad had been positioned as the first pocket-sized tablet computer or the most powerful device you could carry in your pocket, without focusing on the handwriting recognition, it

would have been much more successful. Users would have accepted
the need to print carefully or could have used the onscreen keyboard.
The lesson is that how a product is marketed and positioned can
make or break it.

Public Relations

One of the most effective methods of communicating to the world
about your product is through the use of public relations (PR). Among
many of PR's roles, one of the most important is communicating with
the industry journalists who, through their writings and reporting,
tell their audiences about your product.

Public relations is much more effective than advertising in both the
breadth and quality of the messaging. It's particularly useful for companies on limited budgets. An advertisement touts your own product
and is not perceived as being totally objective. PR, on the other hand,
generates reviews and articles written by experts and is much more
believable.

In the United States and Europe, several hundred people communicate most of the news about new high-tech consumer products. They
include analysts and reviewers for the daily national newspapers,
syndicated news services, local newspapers, weekly and monthly business, computer, and news publications, and the top blogging sites.
That's where your PR activities are focused.

You'll want to meet with the top 10 to 20 of these people as well as
your local newspapers as part of a product introduction. You'll need
to provide samples of shipping-quality products to most reviewers to
get their attention, and it needs to be done before the product goes
on sale, taking into account the lead times for their publications. Ideally the reviews and articles begin as the product becomes available.

Most companies use outside public relations companies that specialize in their industry and have relationships with the influencers in that industry. For high-tech consumer products in the U.S., these influencers include reviewers for the *New York Times*, *USA Today*, the *Wall Street Journal*, *PC World*, *PC Magazine*, *Laptop* magazine, *Business Week*, *Forbes*, *CNet*, and *Wired*, TV networks, as well as the gadget blogs such as Engadget and Gizmodo.

I've worked with many PR companies, both introducing new products and as a columnist reviewing new products they provided. Capabilities and results vary widely among the companies, so making the right selection for your company is at least as important as hiring a high-level employee. My recommendation for small- to medium-sized companies is to choose a small agency where those working for you have had many years of experience. Unless you're a huge business, large agencies are less effective; as a small company, you'll likely be assigned to those with less experience.

You'll want a PR person who can truly understand your product, your customers, and your market as well as you do. You'll want someone with strong communication skills, both verbal and written. And you'll want someone who's able to tell you what you may not want to hear. This person will be your face to much of the outside world and will be talking and writing about your product and company and communicating your messages, as well as listening to what others think about your company and your product.

At Think Outside, our PR agency was Martell Communications of Campbell, California. Their role was to help us launch the company and generate awareness of Think Outside's PDA keyboard—a product that many at first thought there wasn't a market for because of the price. While we expected to be selling and marketing the product through Palm and Targus, we had not finalized agreements. Our product was ready to ship so we moved ahead with our launch.

The agency's first step was to conduct a business press tour with influential media editors, presenting the product, answering questions, and leaving production samples for them to use. For a small company without an advertising budget, these in-person meetings were critical to the success of the launch. We presented our product to ABC, CBS, NBC, CNN, the *New York Times*, *Wall Street Journal*, *San Jose Mercury*, *Business Week*, *PC Magazine*, *PC World*, *USA Today*, *Fortune*, and *Forbes*. With one exception, the response was terrific.

Some grabbed their fellow editors from the newsroom and brought them into the conference room to see the keyboard. At ABC the sample was shown to Ted Koppel who called me with our first order. The one exception to the enthusiastic responses was from one of the most influential technology columnists of all, Walt Mossberg of the *Wall Street Journal*. We knew immediately he might not appreciate the product when he began to use it. He was typing with two fingers. But he was cordial and his review was generally positive.

Meeting with the press is best done when there's a firm ship date, a product that's essentially the same as what will be sold, and locations available where the product can be purchased. There's so much vaporware and delayed introductions in this industry that, with few exceptions, journalists don't want to write about what's not available.

The cost of a PR campaign to launch a new product can range from $50,000 to $150,000 or more. Ongoing PR costs can vary but are typically $5,000 to $15,000 per month for a one- or two-product company.

Customer Service

Poor customer service is a massive problem and getting worse. I'm constantly astounded at how many companies care less about the customer after the sale is made. The Consumerist Web site (www.consumerist.com) is filled each day with horror stories about how poorly customers are treated. They are lied to and deceived, promises to call back rarely occur, and repaired products often are returned in worse shape than when they were sent in.

Too many companies assume the worst of their customers. They make it impossible for them to contact a real person. Instead they're forced to navigate a voicemail system that ends up with someone they can barely understand and who has no authority to do anything. These companies seem to do everything possible to keep customers away, even deeply burying their phone numbers and contact information on their Web sites.

Dell Computer once led the computer industry by providing superior customer service, even sending help to the customer's office or home. Then they began tinkering with their model. They continued to offer free in-home service, but added restrictions that made it difficult to qualify for a visit, requiring the customer to try everything else first, including reinstalling Windows, even when it made no sense. They put the burden on the customer to prove he needed the on-site visit, even though he had paid for it. Dell downgraded their phone support by outsourcing it to poorly trained personnel overseas. They took away what their customers had found most valuable and what Dell had become known for.

In this age of instant communications, word spread quickly, reaching a tipping point when one well-known blogger, Jeff Jarvis, described on his blog (www.buzzmachine.com) the frustrating experience he had trying to get his Dell computer repaired. The story was then picked up by dozens of newspapers, magazines, and blogs.

One of Michael Dell's first steps after returning to run the company has been to improve customer service and bring some of it back to the United States.

Too many companies consider customer support as a cost center, not as a marketing investment. The problem is that the analyses used to calculate the cost of service can't measure the value that a positive customer experience can provide, such as repeat and referral sales.

As a technology columnist I frequently hear from readers asking for help. They bought a defective product and can't get it fixed or replaced, or their product suddenly stopped working, and it costs more to fix than to replace. Yet when a company does the right thing, people are ecstatic, often posting it on the Web for thousands to read. Consumers want to find companies that are respectful and don't make them feel like they were taken advantage of, or worse, deceived.

Problems are common with high-tech products, so companies should plan for dealing with them. Rates of defective units can be in the double digits in the first few months of production. It's the nature of the processes and the learning curves of building, testing, and using these complex devices. The early buyers take the most risk and assume that the company will stand behind the product. The early adopters are often the ones with a preponderance of problems, and they need to be treated well. Not only because they deserve it, but also because they're the most influential. Any early issue immediately shows up on the Internet. Early adopters are the first to write about their experiences. A high defect rate is less of a problem than the lack of providing a positive response to that defect.

When Apple introduced the iPhone they provided superb service. While they never publicized it, defective iPhones were swapped out during the first few months for most any reason. That eliminated disappointed customers who quickly forgot about the problems and, instead, praised Apple. Their positive experiences filled the message boards, seen by the tens of thousands who were waiting and wondering whether to buy.

Sprint is going through a huge loss of customers. It's not that their cellular service is much different than their competition's, it's that their customer service has been the worst among the four major American carriers. It's not as if their competitors are all that good; in fact, with just some decent service and more consumer-friendly policies, Sprint could stand out from the others. Every company executive should try calling their own customer service; many have no idea and would likely be surprised at what they subject their customers to.

At Think Outside we strived for exceptional customer service using a few simple guidelines. A live person who was smart and had good common sense answered all calls; voicemail was used only after working hours or when the phones were busy, and those calls were quickly returned. Those who answered the phone were well trained and had the authority to satisfy the customer by replacing the product. After all, that customer spent $100 of their money to buy our product. How can you not treat them with respect? If anyone asked, they would be put through to me.

Anyone who called to complain about our product not working was asked to return it at our expense. We sent out a replacement the same day they called, before we received their defective unit back. This policy astounded most customers. "You mean you trust that I'll send in my unit?" many would ask. Frankly, I was astounded that they were astounded, but it pointed out how widespread is the attitude of companies not trusting their customers. Sending out a replacement product the same day sent three messages: We wanted to minimize their inconvenience, we valued their business, and we trusted them. The bar has been set so low by so many companies that it's easy to excel in customer service today. It's also the right thing to do.

I had one experience that I'll never forget. A customer called to say that he had a defective keyboard he bought from Palm, and they were unwilling to help. He was angry when he next called Think Outside, asking to speak to the president. His call was put through, and he told me he wanted his money back. I offered to send him a refund, but asked if I could first overnight him a replacement unit, because I wanted him to have a good unit to try. He quickly became more cordial and mentioned he was a dentist in Howard Beach, Queens, New York. I asked him if he knew my late father-in-law who had a medical practice there for many years. The caller seemed stunned for a moment, and then explained that not only did he know my father-in-law, but that he had been his own doctor and was one of the reasons for his getting into medicine.

Establishing Price

One of marketing's functions is to establish the product's price. Price is dependent on the perceived value, the product's cost, and how the product is distributed. When products are more of a commodity or have intense competition, the product is priced to match or beat your competitors. It's an area where the product counts less, and price and promotion count more.

With products that are more differentiable, there's less pressure on pricing. It's usually better to set prices on the high side, particularly in the beginning. The demand is higher, and you need not give up margins at the outset. With the Stowaway priced at $100, several times higher than most full-size keyboards, it still sold briskly for more than a year before we lowered the price.

Users expect the prices of high-tech products to fall over time, so if you need to reduce the price, it won't come as a surprise, even to those that paid the higher price. When Apple set the price of the first iPhone at $599 and sales slowed after the initial demand, they dropped the price by $200 a few months later with no lasting damage. (The early buyers were provided with a $100 store credit).

How a product is distributed affects the amount a product is marked up from its cost to the retail price. As shown in Chapter 3, retail distribution often means the retail price can be as much as 5 times the manufacturing cost. With direct sales through your own Internet site the retail might only be 2 times cost. (Distribution is covered in more detail in Chapter 8, "Distribution: Getting Your Product to the Customer.")

When sales don't meet forecasts, often the first response is to cut the price. That's usually the message you'll get from retailers and your salespeople. But lowering the price does not always improve sales. Many other factors can cause slow sales; often it's lack of customer awareness of the product.

Slow sales too often trigger a response to look for ways to reduce price. One of the most common actions is to ask your supplier to lower his cost to you. Wal-Mart has a reputation of pushing its Asian manufacturers to cut every last penny and set a schedule for reductions over time, and it's an example that other companies have tried to emulate.

My experience, as discussed in Chapter 5, "Why Outsource?" has been that squeezing the last dollar out of the cost can cause more harm than good. Asian suppliers typically work on small margins, but they do like to negotiate. The trick is to know when they've reached a price that provides them with a fair profit, yet not so low that they will lose interest in your business or sacrifice the quality.

Consumer electronics companies put an inordinately heavy emphasis on cutting cost without realizing how hurtful it can be to the product, the manufacturer, and to its workers. I would urge company executives who push for lower pricing to measure the impact of their actions not only at the front end in the marketplace, but also at the back end in the factories.

Many customers would be willing to pay a slightly higher price if they knew that the extra cost went toward providing better conditions for workers and improved product quality. I'd love to see a consumer electronics company offer two identical products side by side as an experiment, but one at a 5% premium with a tag saying the extra cost is going directly into a fund for the workers' care. Which would you buy?

Pricing decisions are not always obvious. An audio client had been selling a high-end earphone model for $400, but sales had reached a plateau. They debated whether to offer a model for $150 with performance that was about 80% as good. They were concerned that it would impact the sales of the $400 product, but decided to proceed, the logic being that it's better that you be the one to offer the best alternative to your product than your competitor. Also it was possible that the lower cost product would bring more attention to the top-of-the-line product. What happened? Sales of the $400 product increased when the $150 product went on sale, and the $150 product became a solid success. Conventional thinking would have lowered the price of the $400 product to increase sales.

CHAPTER 8

Distribution:
Getting Your Product to the Customer

Each time someone touches your product, you incur a cost.

Build it and they will come. That rarely happens. Not only do you need a marketing program, but also a plan to get your product into the marketplace and in the hands of your customers.

What Are Your Choices?

1. Sell your product through retail distribution into real brick and mortar stores (B&M) where your potential customers shop. This requires working with distributors that provide the products to the stores.

2. Supply your product to a marketing company that has established marketing and distribution channels.

3. Sell over the Internet, using both your own site and those of others. This is becoming an increasingly popular choice, particularly for introducing a new product.

4. License your product to another company to design, manufacture, distribute, and receive a royalty on sales.

Retail Distribution

Retail B&M distribution involves selling your product through retail storefronts, such as Best Buy, Staples, Wal-Mart, and RadioShack in the U.S. and Carrefour, FNAC, and Media Markt in Europe.

Retail storefronts make it easy for customers to see, try, and buy. Having the product in these stores creates awareness, promotes sales, and creates legitimacy for the product. How many times have you gone into a store planning to buy just a few items and walked out with a lot more?

While this channel usually offers the biggest upside, nearly all the companies I've worked with have found it to be a frustrating and difficult experience.

With the huge increase in the number of new products competing for the limited shelf space of a decreasing number of retailers, it's only getting more difficult. The customer's experience also has gotten worse, as the customer must decipher more complex products with inexperienced store employees who often have little product knowledge.

At Seiko Instruments I learned firsthand how difficult it was to sell into retail stores. Even with a pristine brand name, Seiko ran into difficulties getting distribution for its consumer electronics and Smart Label printer products. Retailers would require huge up front payments to take the products, insisted that the packaging be tailored just for their stores, took months to pay, and then returned unsold products half a year later. Even Apple struggled. Their retail success blossomed only after they took matters into their own hands and built their own stores, and placed their own employees in other stores such as Best Buy to sell their products.

Rather than selling directly to the stores it's more common to sell through one or more of the major distributors that inventory the product and supply it to the retailers. To determine how best to distribute your products through retailers, you must first identify your target customers, figure out where they will most likely go to buy such a product, and work with the distribution companies that supply products and already have a relationship with these retailers. Some examples of distributors for consumer electronics are Ingram Micro, Tech Data, and D and H. But they won't take your product automatically.

You first must set up a sales call and presentation to convince a distributor to carry your product. Besides product features, functionality, industrial design, and packaging, a distributor will look at the price point of the product, margins you are offering, and what type of marketing and advertising support you will give the product. Once your product is accepted by the distributor, negotiation is required to determine discounts, volume rebates, return policies, payment terms, promotional and marketing payments, and allowances as well as up front payments. Ideally you'd like a distributor with experience in your product category, and who doesn't carry your top competitor's product.

Each of these distributors stocks tens of thousands of different products, and each is set up to efficiently deliver them to the retailers. Retailers prefer to order from distributors rather than from companies that offer just one or two products. It enables them to create a single order for hundreds of products rather than hundreds of orders for a few products from many companies.

Distributors offer many services, including warehousing and product fulfillment, billing and terms to resellers, and in some cases training and marketing for the product. However, don't expect the distributor to do the selling for you. You'll still need to market or promote your products directly to the key retailers. You'll need to work directly with their buyers to convince them to carry your product. It's often a long process with no guarantee of success.

In those cases in which a large retailer has a strong interest in carrying your product, they can be helpful in establishing a relationship with one of the distributors they use.

You may want to enlist the help of a sales rep company, rather than build your own sales organization, particularly in the case of a first product going into new and uncharted markets. Select a sales rep firm that has strong relationships with the particular retailers and buyers you're trying to reach. But don't leave it all to the sales reps; accompany them to the initial meetings with the buyers of new major accounts; you know the product better than anyone and have the most passion and vision to talk about it. The rep will also gain insight on how you position your product during a sales call. A rep takes a percentage of the sale, often 5% to 10%, and sometimes a monthly retainer, as well. Reps need to be managed just as an internal sales force would be managed.

Distribution Costs

Each time someone touches your product you incur a cost. In the distribution model for consumer electronics the retailer may take from 20% to 60% of the retail price. The distributor will take an additional few percent, up to about 10%. The exact amount depends on the type of product, how unique it is, and the market demand for it. Companies offering products with strong demand can often negotiate lower margins.

The experiences of Airzen (an alias) illustrate the challenges of retail distribution. The company's founder, Bob Janzen, invented a product, the AirGo, that's used with a computer to improve the connection speed to the Internet. He began selling it over his Web site, but to achieve a substantial volume of sales, he added distribution into a number of retail chains. His product retailed to the end user for $50, and the wholesale price to the reseller was $30. His cost from the factory was $12, so he made $18 gross profit, the difference between what he paid for it and what he sold it for before the distributor's cut. Seems like a great business, but he quickly found that a huge number of hidden costs ate up much of his profit.

The retailer took an additional 10% (of the $30) for market development funds, reducing Airzen's gross profit from $18 to $15. The distributor took 6.5%, reducing it to $13. At the insistence of the retailer, Janzen had to hire a local rep to manage the relationship; this rep took 4%, reducing the gross profit by another dollar to $12. The distributor took another $.50, called a *volume incentive rebate*. Shipping costs of $1 were paid by Airzen, reducing the margin to $10.50 (see Figure 8.1).

And there's more. The distributor charged $20,000 to set up the initial account with Airzen (negotiated down from $40,000). The retailers imposed numerous charges from time to time for promoting the product. For example, when one ran a holiday sale, it offered a $10 in-store rebate and charged Airzen $6 of that. The distributor also took a 2% discount that he was entitled to if he paid within 20 days, but usually stretched out payments to more than three months.

The creativity of the retailers to extract fees was never-ending. Janzen got an "invitation" to attend a meeting of one of the national retailers selling his product. He was asked to pay $20,000 for the right to display his products, a requirement for continuing to do business with them. He was able to negotiate it to $10,000, but had little choice.

These miscellaneous fees paid to the retailers for shelf space and promotion are called *soft dollars*, and are often more important to them than direct profits from the sale of the product. If you don't pay, you don't play; retailers rarely take a product from a company that doesn't participate. Janzen tried understanding and justifying the myriad of soft dollar requests, but eventually gave up because the explanations were often meaningless.

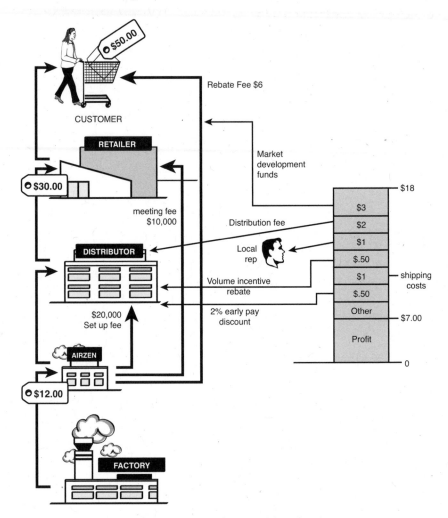

FIGURE 8.1 Airzen's cost of distribution

These soft dollars can also result in excessively large orders by the distributor that are not justified by the actual sales. While it might be exciting to receive, the order size may be motivated by the extra soft dollar income generated, not by the distributor's expectation of actually selling that number of products. After all, the product can be returned with little consequence to the distributor and retailer.

The end result of all these charges was that Airzen's gross profit went from $20 to about $7 for a product that cost $12 to manufacture! That's not a large profit as it needs to cover the company's engineering, marketing, advertising, and all of their other expenses.

Selling Through

Getting your product into a distributor and a retailer is just the first step. It means little if your product sits on the shelves and doesn't sell through. Regardless of the payment terms you've negotiated, consider the product to be on consignment; there's a real possibility it will be returned.

That's a hardship for a company with limited resources and requires carefully monitoring the actual sales and returns at the retailer. You'll want to ensure that you don't overproduce and that you manage your production quantities to match your sales needs. Close contact with the retailers carrying your products is a must. Fortunately, many offer the ability to tap into their computers to access sales figures.

As small, individually owned retail stores are replaced with super-stores, power is concentrated in fewer and fewer retailers that wield enormous influence. Sometimes that makes these fees seem more like extortion.

It can also be difficult for a small company selling just a few products to have influence with a huge retailer, even if the company has a superior product. Companies with a single product are at a huge disadvantage. Your large competitors have enormous budgets and can play hard.

One product company that developed one of the first USB hubs had been successfully selling them to a large computer superstore chain. One day they suddenly found that their orders stopped and the retailer was dropping them. What happened?

Another company developed a line of competitive products and paid the reseller a large fee for exclusivity in this category. Because this company sold a broad line of products and had an established relationship with the reseller, the first company lost out and eventually went out of business.

Lastly, there's another potential cost for categories of products that have some complexity, such as smartphones or routers. They often have returns as high as 20%—not as a result of any defect, but because consumers are unable to get them to work. They may get a replacement from the store only to find the new one "still doesn't work." That means two units will be returned that are perfectly good, but cannot be sold as new.

While this all sounds discouraging, some companies find great success in retail distribution. These are usually companies that carry a broad product line over a large number of categories. These companies make it easy for the retailers. They provide a single source, offering hundreds of products. They manage the inventory of the retailer, and they can afford to provide large incentives. A company with just a single or a few products can also be successful if its products are so unique that they can draw customers into the store. In some cases, the best way to avoid the pitfalls of distribution of a single product, is to let one of the large, multiproduct companies do it for you.

Partner with a Marketing Company

At Think Outside, because of the frustrating experience with consumer retailing that some board members and I had, we looked at alternatives for the Stowaway. Our core competency was inventing and developing products, and then manufacturing them in Asia. That's where it seemed to make the most sense to invest our resources, rather than to pour money into creating a brand name and enduring the costs of retail distribution, particularly with a single product.

As previously noted, we arranged to sell our finished products in different versions to Palm and Targus, each of whom had strong relationships with retailers and had broad worldwide distribution.

While there was a new cost to us, their profit margins, they took on all responsibilities and costs for marketing, distribution, and working with the distributers and resellers. That included advertising, sales, returns, and first-line customer support. We, in turn, were responsible for the design and manufacturing of all the hardware and software, and backup customer support. This approach allowed us to get to market and reach a huge international audience of customers much more quickly, while permitting us to focus on developing follow-on products.

Table 8.1 shows how the financial models of each compare:

TABLE 8.1   Distributing directly versus using marketing companies

	THINK OUTSIDE DISTRIBUTES	USE PALM AND TARGUS TO DISTRIBUTE	COMMENTS
Retail price	$99	$99	Set by market requirements.
Retailer's cost	$74	$78	Smaller than normal margins for retailer, but possible because of demand and uniqueness of the product. Palm and Targus were able to negotiate a smaller dealer margin than we were.
Cost to Palm/Targus	Not applicable	$53	
Our cost	$38	$36	Cost drops as volume increases.
Our gross profit	$36	$17	
Costs for marketing, distribution, sales, support, advertising, and staff	$20	$6	Lower variable marketing costs plus fixed costs spread over much higher volumes.
Our net profit	$16	$11	
Sales volume first year	150,000	600,000	The large differences in volume are a result of Targus and Palm having worldwide distribution, strong brand recognition, and the ability to reach worldwide markets many months sooner than we could.
Gross profit first year	$2.4M	$6.6M	

Operating as a supplier of the product and outsourcing much of the distribution and marketing was an excellent strategy for us and can certainly work well for others. It's something that's done more frequently, as companies with strong distribution channels need a constant stream of new products and look to others to supply them. In the past there was a greater level of NIH (not invented here) in which companies were reluctant to market products from others.

Now those with unique offerings can often find numerous opportunities for these partnerships.

However, such an arrangement requires careful management of these relationships. You need to work with your partners and carefully monitor what they are doing. You need to know how well your product is selling and avoid becoming isolated from what's occurring in the marketplace, even though some companies are reluctant to share this information.

One of the biggest and nearly fatal mistakes we made was assuming that Palm's sales and marketing forecasts were accurate. They provided bullish forecasts to us, and we, in turn, built tooling and ordered parts to support those numbers, never thinking their estimates might be inaccurate. At one point they were placing orders with us for 300,000 units per month when their sales rate was at 100,000.

When Palm's sales of PDAs suddenly slowed down, we were financially impacted from having built too much tooling and ordering too many parts. We were too naïve in believing their numbers. That was our responsibility, and we suffered as a result. Palm had been unwilling to share with us how they developed their forecasts, but we should have been more insistent.

In spite of careful due diligence it's often impossible to know just how well such a relationship will work out. One client developed products that were to be sold by a major accessory marketing company. While they initially showed great enthusiasm and provided good initial forecasts, the business turned out to be a tiny fraction of what was promised. The accessory company went through a reorganization shortly after the client began shipping product, the advocate left, and there was no support for the products from the new organization.

Internet Sales

Selling through the Web is often a good way to get started, particularly selling from your own site. Startup costs are low; it's an opportunity to satisfy early demand, particularly when a product is first being promoted. Profits are also higher because you're avoiding one extra markup. You do have to invest in some marketing to draw traffic to your site, such as PR and online advertising.

Selling directly lets you get close to your customers to gain valuable information. You can find out what customers think about your product, test new ideas, conduct surveys, and discover potential issues.

Your Web site is also a wonderful vehicle for posting press articles, reviews, and awards. A well-designed site provides a bigger-than-life presence that let's you look as substantial and professional as much larger companies.

At Think Outside we conducted frequent online surveys of our customers to find out what they liked best and least and how they used the products. We solicited user stories that provided credible, real-life examples. One was from a mountain climber who used his keyboard to write a daily journal of his adventures. With his permission we added his experience to our Web site along with a picture. We followed up personally with some early customers and used them to test new products.

Once we were in retail distribution, we always sold products over our Web site at the suggested retail price, never undercutting dealers that carried our product. Our goal was not to obtain sales as much as it was a vehicle to promote the product and the locations where it could be purchased.

Today there are many excellent Web sites for selling your product, such as Amazon.com, Buy.com, jr.com, cdw.com, Newegg.com, Bestbuy.com, Costco.com, and so on. Unlike your own site, they work on similar margins as bricks and mortar stores, and obtain their products through the same distributors. There are also many no-name resellers with Web sites run out of a home or small office, with low overhead and no customer support, simply shipping the product directly from the distributor. While they can increase sales, you'll want to guard against them cutting prices too much. You don't want to undercut retailers that provide service and support and make the effort to explain and promote your product.

Pricing, sales, and distribution are closely related. You might think that the more stores that carry your product the more sales you will make. But that's rarely the case. If your product is found everywhere it's more likely that some of the stores will heavily discount it, and many more will fail to promote it and then will drop it for the lack of profitability. That often results in fewer sales over the long term.

Ideally you want to sell into fewer stores, but you must choose those stores wisely, avoiding those that sell close to their cost. While you can't dictate what price they'll sell it for, you have the right to sell to whomever you want and to provide assistance to help them be successful. That encourages them to carry, support, and promote your products.

Internet sales don't allow the customer to touch and try your product before buying and don't provide the same level of exposure as the storefronts. Many Internet sales result from seeing the product at retail and then ordering it online to save money. For many companies, Internet sales are still a small fraction of their total sales. But sales over the Internet will continue to grow over time because of the convenience, efficiency, price advantage, and helpful information that's often available. I shop at Amazon frequently, because it's become a pleasant experience. I can check reviews of a product I'm interested in, pay a competitive price, and receive the product within a day or two, often with free shipping.

Licensing

Licensing is another way to take your idea and get it to market. It's an arrangement in which you offer your invention to another company to manufacture, market, and distribute, and sometimes even design. In return you're paid a percentage of sales, typically from a few percent to as much as 10% of the wholesale price, depending on the uniqueness, patentability, and potential. Usually there's an up front payment to the inventor as an advance against royalties. Licensing generally works best if you have a single product and do not have the experience, funds, or resources to perform all the other activities from engineering to marketing.

At Seiko we licensed the label printer concept from an independent inventor. He received a percentage of the price Seiko sold it for, which began at 4% and decreased to zero after several years. In this case the advantage of the licensing agreement to the inventor was that he didn't need to take the product beyond the concept stage and didn't need to make any further investment.

One of the risks for the inventor is that the company may choose not to develop the product, take a long time to bring it to market, or just do a poor job designing or marketing the product. The inventor may also lose control over how the product is developed and commercialized. A licensing arrangement requires a detailed contract that provides some safeguards to minimize these occurrences.

CHAPTER 9

Legal Advice: Knowing When to Ignore It

A successful relationship is based less on having tight legal agreements and more on finding a company with high integrity.

As an engineer by training, I was unprepared to adequately judge many of the legal activities in which I became involved. We learn about thinking in terms of right and wrong, black and white. And isn't that what law is all about? Far from it!

Over the years I've learned a lot and formed some strong opinions, not all positive. I experienced all sorts of legal challenges that I've been told are typical for companies with popular products. But looking back, I found much of the advice from capable lawyers in prestigious law firms to be impractical and just plain wrong. And if I had to do it over, I think I'd be better off without so much legal advice, and I would have saved a lot of money.

Patents

I used to believe that patents were critically important to protecting an invention. That's the way I was trained. At Polaroid I received many patents for all sorts of inventions, some that were commercialized, but many that were not. For example, I developed a variety of methods to dispense developer fluid onto film. While just one of the many methods was used in the product, all the others were patented as a defensive strategy to prevent other companies from utilizing them. This was an area of critical importance to Polaroid, whose core competency was applying developer to film in a variety of ways. This strategy helped perpetuate Polaroid's monopoly in instant photography. When Kodak introduced competing instant cameras and film, they were sued by Polaroid, and after a long battle, had to exit the business and pay a huge fine for violating Polaroid's patents. This experience may explain my original awe of patents.

Now, while patents are still important to companies developing products with core technologies such as microprocessors, software technology, and biotech, their value to many consumer products is often much less.

That's because much has changed in today's consumer world, where products are developed in months instead of years and can last less than a year in the market rather than several. Applying for patents for these products may not be a good investment of your time or funds, nor may they have any lasting value. Their utility is even more uncertain with the current disarray in the patent system.

Placing false hope on patents can drain a company of its resources and focus. I've encountered many inventors who invested tens of thousands of dollars in applying for patents in dozens of countries. They often consider the patent to be their key to success. While it may make them feel better and stoke their egos, patents often provide false security.

First, it can take several years for the patent to be issued. During this "patent pending" period, until a patent is granted, you can't prevent another company from copying your ideas. So you might have invented a clever product, applied for patents, and then faced competition. And with shorter development times, a company can often introduce a competing product in months, years before your patent will even be issued! By the time your patent does issue, both you and your competitor's products may no longer even be on the market.

Even when your patent is granted, it's rare that you can stop an infringing company from selling its product. You'll have to challenge the company in court, and that can take years and cost hundreds of thousands of dollars. Your only recourse is to obtain an injunction to halt the company's sales, but injunctions are not easily granted.

Even when you go to market with a patent already issued and in hand, its value can still be limited. When we developed our first keyboard at Think Outside and were about to begin production, we discovered a patent that had just been published but was still a few months from being issued. It described a folding keyboard that had some similarities to our product. Why didn't our lawyer find this when he was conducting a search? Because the US Patent Office doesn't publish patent applications, only those about to be issued.

This actually turned out to be a positive development. It offered us a chance to license the patent from the inventor and have immediate protection without waiting for our own patents to be issued. We contacted the inventor, an entrepreneur in London, who had been working on a similar concept for several years. He was unable to solve some of the technical problems and had abandoned his efforts to commercialize the idea. But he did go ahead and file a patent. We quickly came to an agreement, and for a royalty, received exclusive rights to his patent.

But we soon learned that even having patent protection from day one didn't prevent other companies from coming to market. While it gave us about a nine-month advantage and put us in a stronger negotiating position with Palm and Targus, its value was short-lived.

As we received more publicity and won numerous awards, including *PC Magazine*'s product of the year, other companies identified this category as one ripe for entry. We were performing their market testing and proved that there was a market.

One of the consequences of instant communications over the Internet is that a hot product almost anywhere in the world creates immediate awareness and stokes other companies to jump in and compete. If a product is successful, you can usually expect to see knock-offs or variations of it in months. And it's not as if we didn't see this coming; within a few days of our product introduction we saw a huge number of hits to our Web site from Chinese, Taiwanese, Korean, and Japanese addresses.

Patent or no patent, others found a way to develop competing products. We thought we were clever, but others came up with equally clever solutions without violating our patent. The lesson we learned is that even though we had a patent from the day the product came to market, it failed to keep out competition. Moreover, it created a false confidence that we were protected.

The patent strategy a company pursues depends on a number of factors. If you're developing consumer products that can be brought to market quickly and easily emulated, the value of a patent is minimal. On the other hand if you're developing products that are the result of years of research and have a long life, patents may have significant value, particularly when the company behind the product has the resources to defend it.

With respect to consumer electronic products, the best way to protect your intellectual property is to keep improving your product and fight it out in the marketplace. Don't count on patents to protect you from competition. Instead, put yourself in the position of one of your competitors. Look at your products through their eyes and try to figure out how to make the next one more attractive, better performing, and less expensive. That's what every company should be doing with its own products. Invent follow-on products that are the best competitive products to your own.

The other issue of patents is when you are at the receiving end of a patent infringement lawsuit. Think Outside was in discussions with another company to manufacture its product, but when sales slowed we broke off discussions. Nothing had been signed nor had any commitment been made. That company, a Japanese-based keyboard manufacturer, threatened to sue us for patent infringement if we did not use them as a manufacturer. They claimed ownership of a patent on a certain type of key switch. Our patent lawyers examined their patent and could find no relevance. Yet that didn't stop them from suing. Clearly it was a reprisal lawsuit. We were unable to have the suit dismissed, as it was not obvious to the judge that there was no infringement. The suing company tried every maneuver it could to make our lives miserable. Finally, after more than two years of rulings and appeals, the company lost. Our lawyers were elated that we had won. So, just what was winning? Spending more than a million dollars that we couldn't afford. But to our lawyers, who ended up with a part of that million dollars, that was winning!

Before investing heavily in a new product development it's important to find out if your design conflicts with patents that have already been issued. That requires a patent search that can be done by lawyers or yourself using the online resources of the Patent Office (www.uspto.gov).

When scanning the patents, pay most attention to the numbered claims at the end of a patent. Even if the rest of the patent sounds like your product, what really counts is what the claims say. If you do find patents that cover your design you'll need to either design around them or license the patent.

Agreements and Contracts

Now if you think I'm skeptical about patents, let me tell you about agreements and contracts. As noted, Think Outside relied on marketing our products through companies that already had brand names and worldwide marketing and distribution. One of those companies was Palm, which at the time had the largest market share of PDAs (personal digital assistants), the ideal match for our keyboard. Users could snap a Palm into our keyboard and experience the benefits of a pocket-sized computer.

We entered into negotiations with Palm and concluded a contract that designated Think Outside as the exclusive provider of keyboards to Palm in return for our not selling a Palm version to anyone else, other than over our Web site. It was an agreement that worked for several years during which two million units were sold, and it became one of the best-selling PDA accessories ever. We continued to work with Palm and developed two follow-on models, a premium product called the XT and a lower cost bifold design called the IR that used infra-red to communicate, rather than using a connector. Both were sold under a similar contract with mutual exclusivity. Each time we renewed the contract it cost several tens of thousands of dollars in legal fees. Our lawyer liked to negotiate, although in the end we signed something similar to what we had started with.

One day, Palm informed us that they had developed their own folding keyboard that was a near copy of our IR keyboard. They informed us that they'd no longer be buying our IR model but would continue to buy the XT. What could we do? Our lawyer talked about suing them for infringement and breech of contract, but Palm was also our customer, in fact, our biggest customer. How practical was that? After much discussion with our board members and key investors we concluded that suing was not a practical option. We would need to spend a huge amount of money for an uncertain outcome, while losing sales of the other product they were buying.

So, another lesson learned. Contracts are useful. They spell out terms and conditions of a relationship, but a small company has little recourse should a large partner change their mind. That's not a reason for not doing contracts, but don't believe they'll solve all your problems.

Development and Manufacturing Agreements

Some of your most important agreements will be with an Asian partner, who will typically provide development and manufacturing services, turning your ideas into manufacturable products. These agreements define many of the details and responsibilities. I've worked with many law firms to create a variety of these agreements. Most lawyers are firm believers in their importance and usually advise that to minimize risk it's best to complete the agreements before beginning work. But in today's new environment where fast to market is so critical, that's usually not practical, particularly with Asian companies, where agreements need to go through translations and can take a long time to conclude.

To wait for an agreement to be signed before engaging a partner can seriously impact your time to market. That's usually not something your lawyer or CFO may be comfortable with, but it's frequently a requirement for fast development.

I was challenged with questions such as: "How can you provide a payment to get them started on development without an agreement?" Or, "What if they don't do what they say they will do?" While there's certainly a small risk, it's a lot less of a risk than delaying the schedule during the time it takes to conduct the usual back-and-forth negotiations to complete an agreement.

The worst case is that you'll lose an initial payment, but wouldn't you like to know that the company is disreputable or unable to produce your product sooner rather than later? In all my years, working with dozens of companies, I've never had that happen. Most Asian OEM and ODM suppliers are interested in your business because they can keep their factories running by producing your product. None I've encountered have ever had any interest in unfairly profiting from the development activities.

Furthermore, the value of legal agreements to Asian companies is much less important than to us. They have fewer lawyers and have a much less litigious legal system. Many are willing to begin work on a handshake, a pleasant change from the way business is conducted in the United States and Europe.

When I managed the development of the Newton MessagePad, I was under intense pressure to bring out a second-generation model that corrected some of the deficiencies of the first. The first product was being built by Sharp in Japan. It was expensive and had numerous design defects, not uncommon in first-generation products. My goal was to find a new company to do the production development and manufacturing at a lower cost, yet with the capability to complete the development in ten months. I gave myself one month to find that company.

I scoured Asia, traveling to Japan, Taiwan, Korea, and Hong Kong, to find the ideal company. After meeting with a dozen companies in less than two weeks, I narrowed the selection to a few candidates, visited them a second time, and then selected Inventec, a designer and manufacturer of notebook computers and advanced calculators at the time. We now had nine months left.

We began work on the product immediately, since that was the only way we had a chance to meet our target. If we waited for agreements to be completed, that would have taken two to three months, time that could never be made up. We immediately began the development while the lawyers began, in parallel, to structure the development and manufacturing agreements. (Details of what these agreements cover follow.)

There were still a huge number of unknowns. We didn't know the development costs or what the final product cost would be, but, nevertheless, we developed guidelines and moved forward on a handshake. I explained to Richard Lee, the company's president at the time, that I was likely putting my job on the line and was counting on their ability to deliver. My confidence was well-placed, and they delivered on schedule. (Unfortunately, the 30,000/month forecast turned out to be only 3,000/month, but Inventec never asked for a pricing adjustment. Richard taught me about working with honorable companies and the value of a handshake.) In fact, it took about six months to complete the agreements, and we never referred to them again after they were signed.

When development times are 18 to 24 months long, completing these agreements before starting might be more practical, but not when the development times are just 6 or 9 months. The risk of encountering a legal complication or misunderstanding that can't be solved is a lot less than the risk of being late to market. Put the effort into selecting a good supplier and then place your confidence in that supplier without needing a contract to begin.

I've found that sound relationships are not based on having tight legal agreements, but the result of finding a good company with the right skills and a management team with high integrity. Find a company you can trust, establish the details of the business relationship at the start, and then move on. In fact, in the cases in which I've encountered problems with a supplier, they usually occurred because of some other factors, such as a weak team or loss of interest.

So, what's the best way to enter into such a relationship and begin without any detailed agreements? First execute an NDA (nondisclosure agreement). That's a relatively simple form that says what you tell them is confidential and should not be disclosed to others. A mutual NDA is one that works two ways, keeping the information they disclose confidential as well. NDAs are common and make both sides feel a little better. After signing hundreds I've never seen one result in a lawsuit because proving a violation is so difficult.

Once you've identified a partner, outline the relationship by defining in general terms what's expected from each side. It can be done in just a couple of pages. In the case of Inventec we came to the following understanding:

1. Apple to provide the industrial design and electronics design. Inventec to provide the mechanical design, circuit board design, mechanical engineering, tooling, and design of the equipment used to put the product together and to test it.

2. Cost to be calculated based on a formula applied to the bill of materials. (The issue of cost was addressed in a way that reduced surprises or risk. We agreed to establish the final cost based on the cost of the individual components, which could be determined objectively. At this early stage it was impossible to estimate the final product cost, as few of the design details had been established. Apple's cost would be a simple function of what went into the product, and Inventec's profit would be a fixed percentage based on the cost of the parts.)

We then drafted these details into a single-page letter of understanding, rolled up our sleeves, and went to work. Simultaneously our lawyers began creating two agreements, one for the development phase and a second for the manufacturing.

The development agreement defines the details of the development phase and typically includes the following items:

1. **Product specifications**—Defines the details of the product.

2. **Development schedule**—Provides the detailed schedules and milestones from the beginning to the start of production.

3. **Each company's development obligations**—List of activities and the responsible parties.

4. **Development costs and payment milestones**—Charges for the development activities and when they are due.

5. **Ownership of new inventions arising from the development**—Usually inventions and improvements to the product created by the manufacturing partner belong to the product company contracting the work. Manufacturing inventions belong to the manufacturer. (In the case of using a company to build a product based on their own pre-existing technologies or products, the ownership of the design usually remains with that company.)

6. **Indemnification**—Who is responsible for lawsuits from a third party. Normally each company protects the other for the elements they contribute from being challenged by a third company.

7. **Dispute resolution**—Describes how and where any contractual disputes are to be resolved.

8. **Confidentiality**—Describes the confidentiality arrangements between the two companies.

The manufacturing agreement defines the terms of manufacturing and typically includes these items:

1. **Product specifications**—Defines the details of the product.

2. **Engineering change orders**—Describes the process for making changes to the product once production begins.

3. **Quality requirements**—Describes the product's performance in all the important areas.

4. **Inspection and acceptance**—Describes how the product is inspected and what constitutes acceptance. Describes procedures and equipment used for testing.

5. **Order forecasting**—Describes the lead time requirements for ordering product to be manufactured, the requirements for longer range forecasting, and the conditions under which changes can be made.

6. **Epidemic failure definition and resolution**—Describes the conditions under which the manufacturer is responsible for repairing or replacing product that is manufactured and shipped that has a single defect over more than a given percentage of the product that arises from an error in manufacturing or the use of noncomplying parts.

7. **Payment terms**—Describes how the product is paid for.

8. **Product cost**—Describes the product cost.

9. **Intellectual property ownership**—Describes the ownership of the design and manufacturing processes.

10. **Delivery terms**—Describes the terms of delivery. Where it's shipped from, how it's shipped, and how the information is communicated.

11. **Warranties**—Defines the start and length of the product warranty from the manufacturer. It often starts 90 days after receipt of product to allow for time to reach the end customer. One year is typical from the end of the 90 days.

12. **Dispute resolution**—Describes how and where any contractual disputes are resolved.

13. **Confidentiality**—Describes the confidentiality arrangements between the two companies.

One area where a legal agreement is particularly important is with the engineering consultants hired to work on the design. It's important for there to be a clear understanding of ownership of the designs that result from this relationship. Normally the contracting company maintains ownership as a result of paying for the work.

Should a product be highly successful you'll want to avoid those who contributed to it from coming back and claiming they should receive added compensation. That's something that occurs all too often, because the original relationship was not clearly spelled out.

As you can see, legal issues permeate the activities of any business. My advice is to be selective in how you use legal services rather than accepting legal advice blindly. But most of all, focus on your product and the schedule and find partners whom you can trust. Get good legal advice, but don't count on patents or agreements to substitute for good business sense.

CHAPTER 10

Now What?

The adventure along the way is personally more rewarding than reaching the finishing line.

When we finally shipped the Stowaway keyboard we all breathed a sigh of relief. After coming up with the idea, raising money, building a team, engineering the product, and then shepherding it through manufacturing, and finding and negotiating with our partners, could we find time to relax?

Perhaps for a long weekend. While we had completed our first product, that was just the beginning. Having a successful product attracted a lot of attention—not just from customers, but also from competitors around the world. After all, almost anything a company does of any importance quickly finds its way onto the Internet!

Companies around the world are constantly looking to find ways to grow, and when they spot a success, some will try to develop their own solutions—everything from blatant copies to similar products with more features, a lower price, or some other variant.

There are many companies whose business model is simply to copy others' products. So expect it. It's not personal; it's business. And it usually happens sooner than you think.

While it seems unfair that others can profit from all your original work and creativity, it's inevitable in the consumer electronics space (as well as most other product areas). If you've applied for patents, its unlikely they've been issued yet, so the best you can do is note "patent pending" on your product.

While you need to be wary of others entering the market, you cannot allow it to distract you. I've worked with executives who would obsess when they saw an announcement or read a rumor about a competing product. It's not healthy, and having new competition is just a fact of life. Your energy is best applied to focusing on what you can control, not what you can't.

Focus on how you can compete with your own products and then go on to develop the best follow-on ones that you can. After all, you know your product best, and you know what compromises you had to make. Use that to your advantage.

In fact, you should be thinking about your next product even before the first one reaches the market, and you should design the first, knowing that it will be upgraded or replaced.

The best defense to competition is developing your follow-on product while your competitors are busy copying your current one, so that you keep one generation ahead. When they come out with a copy of the first, you'll be introducing your new and improved version.

Product sales typically follow a Gaussian curve, one in which the rate of sales first grows quickly, then flattens out, and finally decreases. That may be hard to believe when you're on the steep upward slope, but it's true with nearly every consumer product ever made. As your rate of sales begins to slow down, but before it flattens, introduce a second model with more features, but at a similar price as the first product, while lowering the price of the original model. Because consumers expect to see price reductions, the best way to hold your price is to add features. We see this in all segments of consumer electronics: faster processors, more memory, smaller sizes, software improvements, improved displays, and more. By planning for this during the first product's design process you can reduce the cost of retooling and quickly broaden your line without a large investment. Customers like to have a choice of a few different models that meet certain price points. But don't provide so many choices that it becomes difficult for them to make a purchasing decision. I like having good, better, and best models that allow customers to have several understandable choices.

Product reviewers for newspapers, magazines, TV, radio, and the Internet love to cover new products but have little interest in reviewing one a second time. They've moved on to something else. It's almost impossible for an older product to garner the same level of publicity after its time has passed. But when a product is upgraded it can generate new interest and more press exposure.

One client, a brilliant engineer, took pride that his five-year-old product was still better than his competitors' newest models. But his competitors' products were receiving the reviews and publicity, while his product was long forgotten. Being better was not enough to prevent the newcomers from cutting into his sales, in large part because they were newer, not better, and had more publicity. Consumers are conditioned to think that newer always means better, even when that's not the case.

Companies also add new models for different retailers, or at least try to make the customer think that's the case. Costco might sell a Panasonic HDTV that's essentially identical to one sold by Best Buy, yet they each have different model numbers. That's done, in part, to confuse the customer into thinking there's enough differences for one store to price its model differently from the other. However, I don't think this practice fools most savvy shoppers, especially those who use the Internet to do their research.

Some companies offer "special edition" or "professional" models to full-price retailers such as department stores to enable them to compete with the discount stores. They'll often come with a longer guarantee, a carrying case, or other accessories.

Often models are created to offer products at key price points such as $49, $79, and $99, or $149, $199, and $299. Note that Apple has iPod models at each of these prices.

How often do you need to upgrade your product? Many companies do it every six months or every year, often tying the introduction to major trade shows for their industry.

We thought we would have a year before experiencing serious competition after introducing the Stowaway. But we made a mistake in assuming that our competition would be only those products with similar performance to ours, a full-size keyboard that worked as well as a notebook. Instead we saw keyboards that were smaller and flimsy, but had simpler designs and were less expensive.

One of our board members, who had extensive retailing experience, asked what our plans were for expanding our line. My partner, who invented the product, seemed surprised and explained we already had the best possible product at a fair price. We couldn't compromise and come out with something inferior. It would hurt our reputation and customers would think less of us, and, most of all, it would compromise his principles of only doing exceptional and worthwhile products.

As it turned out, our board member was on to something. After all, we weren't just selling to the consumer; we were selling to the retailer. While Think Outside created a new category, others would be rushing out products and promoting them to the retailers to sell alongside ours or even in place of ours. The retailers were less interested in which model performed best. They wanted to sell more products in this hot new category. What was important to them was the product's price point and profit margin. They knew that some customers shop on price and would settle for a lesser product at a lower cost.

And that's exactly what happened. Others came out with products for $29, $39, $49, $79, and $99. Most were difficult to type with, but that didn't stop the retailers from carrying them and customers from buying them, based on price. While some found them adequate, many did not, but because they were so cheap, they never bothered to return them.

Some of our competition was brazen. We developed software, downloadable from our Web site, that would enable the keyboard to work with new PDAs. One competitor had no time to do their own software; they just sent their customers to our Web site with instructions on using ours. A year later one company, a major keyboard manufacturer, developed an entirely different design that was as clever as ours and worked equally as well.

A dilemma that many companies face after introducing a significant new product is whether to grow the company by working in the same category or to expand into another area of expertise.

There's no correct answer; it depends on what you want your business to become. Do you want to be a dominant market leader in one category, or do you want to jump into a different category where you think you can hit another home run? Do you want to be a market-focused company or an invention company?

Expanding in a given area is generally the less risky choice if you can become a leading player. With more products you can increase market share and increase the efficiency of your operations.

Think Outside's goals were to invent significant new products in the mobility category and not to become the dominate maker of folding keyboards. While it was an important category, we thought folding keyboards would eventually become a commodity with shrinking margins. We didn't think there was an opportunity to make significant improvements after developing the next few models and chose not to develop inferior models. This is a much riskier strategy, but offers the potential of greater rewards if the company can come up with another hit product.

Think Outside used its knowledge of keyboard mechanisms and mechanical engineering skills to create an ingenious PDA, called Polo (see Figure 10.1). It was the same size as those being sold by the market leaders Compaq, H-P, and Palm. Yet it had a built-in folding keyboard that provided full-size keys for touch typing.

FIGURE 10.1 Polo prototype PDA with folding full-size keyboard

Polo was a huge undertaking because it required entirely new skills; we had to add resources needed to design handheld electronic devices with wireless capabilities. We raised additional investment capital and hired new engineers. We eventually entered into an arrangement with Hewlett-Packard for us to build the product, using a Taiwan manufacturer, and for Hewlett-Packard to market it. Over the next nine months we successfully engineered the product and built 75 working models. But one evening I read on the Internet that Hewlett-Packard announced it intended to acquire Compaq. I had a sinking feeling; I knew that with mergers and acquisitions, personnel and priorities change. And that turned out to be the case.

Once the acquisition finally went through many months later, Compaq was given responsibility for all handheld products, H-P's handheld division was closed, and our Polo champion at H-P left the company. Polo was cancelled before ever going into production. While we received a small settlement, it was insufficient to prevent Think Outside from eventually downsizing and being acquired by another company, Mobility Electronics. A year later they discontinued selling the keyboards.

Once a company has developed a successful product there's sometimes the possibility of selling the company to another. Many companies need products to add to their own lines, and an acquisition can provide a source of new products on an ongoing basis.

If you're experiencing success with your first product it's not always easy to objectively consider this option, particularly when you're so close to the business and the product. We're taught that optimism is important in a struggling, growing company, so we're inclined not to consider any downside. Staying the course is familiar and often the easier choice, because it's closest to not making a choice. Selling may mean laying off employees, adding uncertainty about the future, and reining back some of those grand ambitions.

But some companies don't have a second act. Many companies I've worked with wished they had sold when their business was at its peak. A year later, when they were struggling to replicate their initial success, there were no buyers. Unless you have your heart set on building a company, sometimes selling is the best choice. It certainly would have been for Think Outside. The popularity of consumer electronic products is short-lived, just as the lives of companies that produce them can be.

What I've tried to impart in this book is that going from a concept to the consumer requires a series of diverse and multi-faceted activities. When you begin you never know what the outcome will be. For many, including myself, the adventure along the way is personally more rewarding than reaching the finish line. The journey is full of surprises and difficult decisions, but enduring helps us grow and become stronger professionals, and through our mistakes we learn what works and what doesn't. Hopefully, you'll learn from my experiences and mistakes and be a little smarter. After all, life is about learning, and there's clearly no better way to learn than taking one of these trips from concept to consumer.

The Future of Product Development

We've seen a huge transformation in product development over the past 20 years. Development times and product life cycles have gone from years to months. Engineering and manufacturing resources have moved from around the corner to around the world. Sales have moved from a large number of stores to just a few chains and the Internet. Asian skills have grown from building boom boxes to building computers and sophisticated cell phones.

What's in store for the future?

Product development will continue to become more efficient as the building blocks, namely the memory, processors, multifunction chips, and displays, become more powerful and less costly. More companies will be able to create more sophisticated products in less time and at less cost.

Products will become even smaller as circuits will do more with fewer and tinier components. They will consume less power as processors improve and as new displays become more efficient. Displays will roll up and fold, allowing pocket-sized products to expand when used.

Wireless connectivity will be built into products, enabling them to do much more than they do now, including repairing themselves and changing their functionality based on your needs. They'll communicate with one another and with servers to exchange information. GPS technology, already imbedded in cell phones, will be built into cameras, notebooks, and devices of all types, providing information, services, and advertising with the content based on where you happen to be.

Asia, and particularly China, will do more of the design work, while more US and European companies will set up design offices there to get closer to the factories and their new Asian customers. Western companies will continue to play a leading role in innovation, but many need to do a better job at adapting to the changes. Too many are still bureaucratic, unimaginative, and set in their ways, which opens the door for Asian companies to make inroads in their business.

How do we compete? Be more focused on design and marketing of innovative products that customers will want, even if they don't yet know it. Create a climate within the companies that encourages change and the freedom to do things in new ways.

Some of the manufacturing of technology products will migrate from China to other countries such as Vietnam and Indonesia as those countries' infrastructures expand and as China's costs increase, repeating history as when manufacturing moved from Japan to Taiwan to China.

Improvements in how materials and products move from the factory to the customer will reduce the time between manufacturing and sales. Products will flow directly from the factory to the customer within a couple of days of it being ordered and within one day of being manufactured. The supply chain will become a round trip with products returning to their origin for recycling and reuse.

Sales over the Internet will grow, driven by the need to reduce reliance on the inefficient retail distribution system and to allow product companies to get even closer to their customers. Improved Internet experiences with virtual salesrooms that replicate the best of the in-store shopping experience will do a better job of presenting and explaining new products. As long as there are imaginative individuals with ideas and the drive, we're destined to see products we can't even imagine today.

Top Ten Rules

For Taking Your Product from Concept to Consumer

1. Success depends on so much more than just having a great product. Build it and they will come rarely works.

2. Manage your development using a small, focused, cross-functional team with a strong product manager, and with authority to make decisions quickly.

3. Be as creative in the development process as you are with the invention itself.

4. Don't obsess over developing the perfect product. Being early to market is often more important.

5. Market test your product using simple, common sense approaches such as talking to and watching how potential customers work. Go with your gut, but do some sanity checks along the way.

6. Do what you do best and let other companies do what they do best. Don't reinvent what has already been done.

7. Think like your competitor. Plan your next product while doing the first. Then offer the best competitive response to your own product.

8. Understand the sales and distribution channels you'll be using and make sure your product costs allow for a competitive selling price.

9. Monitor sell-through and manage your supply chain closely. Avoid building huge inventories of parts or products before you know how well your product will sell. It's better to be out of stock than overstocked.

10. Don't believe your own hype.

Products and the Environment

This is an amazing time for new gadgetry of all sorts—from flat-panel TVs to printers, from digital cameras to computers. But the rapid advances bring about much shorter product lives. Many of us are on to our fourth printer or second flat-panel TV.

This means that we're replacing products more frequently and inadvertently creating a huge stream of electronic waste (*e-waste*). We're scrapping 400 million electronic products each year in the United States alone. Where do all the old products go that are not passed down to others? Only 13% are recycled, while 87% end up as waste.

That 87% represents 2.3 million tons of e-waste being dumped into landfills or going into incinerators to be burned. E-waste contains lead, mercury, cadmium, and other chemicals used in the production of electronics that are toxic to humans and harmful to our environment. The tube on an old TV or computer monitor contains several pounds of lead. LCD monitors and TVs have mercury lamps that contain dangerous levels of the substance.

While recycling may seem like a good solution, it has its own problems. Much of the electronics brought to recycling centers is exported to China, India, and Africa where workers dismantle the products by hand, separating the waste into piles of plastic, metal, and glass. Recyclers can make a lot more money by sending the e-waste to these countries than by recycling locally using safer methods.

This practice also poses huge problems for the workers. Tests conducted in one community in China found that 80% of the people had lead poisoning, and many had ingested dangerous levels of toxic fire retardants used in the manufacturing process. One town now has to truck in its own water, as the local supply is undrinkable. Waste is often burned next to schools and farms extending their poisonous reach to the neighboring population and to agricultural exports.

Many designers and engineers are now taking into consideration the materials they use, reducing those that are harmful and using more that are recyclable. They're also designing products that make it easier to remove the harmful parts during recycling.

Companies can play an important role in creating better products and assisting in the recycling. Herman Miller, the office furnishings company, has been a pioneer in this area, beginning 30 years ago. They've developed practices that address all aspects of their business, including establishing environmentally responsible design standards for both new and existing products, designing their packaging for efficient use of materials and minimal waste, manufacturing their products using less energy, and constructing and maintaining their building facilities to use less energy. They also provide help to other companies to develop similar policies.

Qualcomm, whose focus is developing chips for mobile phones and other portable devices with extremely low power consumption, has applied that goal to their buildings. They've built a new, combined office building and data center that contains a cogeneration plant to use the heat given off from the servers to partially power the building, reducing energy costs by 39 percent and saving $2.9 million per year.

A number of companies have established policies to take back their products. Dell has the most progressive program among the computer companies. A Dell customer goes online, enters the product's name and serial number, and prints out a postage paid label to send the equipment back. Sony has a program that takes back its televisions at recycling centers.

Staples is the first large U.S. retailer to offer the recycling of old computers in all its U.S. stores. It takes back all brands in addition to monitors, laptops, printers, and fax machines, even if purchased elsewhere.

In the future products will be labeled with environmental information such as the hazardous materials used and the manufacturer's recycling policy, so that we can make an intelligent purchase based on how responsible the manufacturer is. Retailers can begin to do this now, and product reviewers in newspapers, magazines, and on the Internet can include the recycling policies of the companies and products they cover. I've started doing this in my reviews at www.sddt.com/phil and have been encouraging others to do it, as well. We need awareness in the stores, online, and in print.

Designing for the environment provides a huge opportunity for engineers in the United States and Europe to develop new products that are respectful of the environment. It's a new challenge that requires us to use our ingenuity and innovative skills, areas in which we have always excelled. Hopefully, in the future a product's success will be judged not only by its performance and how well it sells, but also by its impact on the environment.

China—Helpful or Harmful?

Considering the impact that China has on our lives and country there is a huge misunderstanding when it comes to manufacturing there. A common belief is that China is taking away our jobs because they use underpaid labor to make poor quality goods.

There's no question that many of our jobs have moved to China. In fact, entire factories have relocated. And there's no doubt that it's resulted in a serious hardship for many, particularly those working in lower level manufacturing jobs. But China's manufacturing capabilities have also had a positive impact on domestic companies.

Each of the activities required to take an idea and bring it to market, as described in the pages of this book, adds value to the process and requires skilled resources to implement.

Philips, Hewlett-Packard, Dell, Motorola, and thousands of other consumer electronics companies invest millions to develop their brands, conduct research, and engineer new products, as part of the development process. Once the product is manufactured they invest millions in distribution, marketing, and after-sale service and support. But the manufacturing that is done in China at relatively low cost actually adds less value than these other activities, because it costs less to do.

In the July/August 2007 issue of the *Atlantic Monthly*, James Fallows, a noted author and journalist, described the relationship of the value added at each stage as the "smiley curve, named for the U-shaped arc of the 1970s-era smiley-face icon, and it runs from the beginning to the end of a product's creation and sale."

Fallows notes, "In case the point isn't clear: Chinese workers making $1,000 a year have been helping American designers, marketers, engineers, and retailers making $1,000 a week (and up) earn even more. Plus, they have helped shareholders of U.S.-based companies."

Examples are everywhere. While I write this, I'm sitting in a Taiwan office tower, Taipei 101, one of the tallest buildings in Asia. Within view in its shopping mall is a Bose retail store, an American company, selling audio equipment made in China. Bose, like many others companies, has prospered from being able to build products at low cost and sell them at a premium.

For example, Bose noise-reducing earphones, so popular with business travelers, retails for $350. Their manufacturing cost is estimated to be $35 to $40, and the factory's profit is perhaps $8. But the gross profit to Bose is more than $300. That means only about 3% of the gross profit stays in China, while the rest comes back to Bose, allowing them to build a highly visible brand, expand their research and development in the United States to design more products, hire more marketers and salespeople, place more ads in newspapers and in other media, and build more retail stores.

The low cost of manufacturing also allows smaller companies that otherwise could not afford to invest in factories to build their own products by outsourcing them to manufacturers skilled in the same areas of expertise. These companies heavily invest in idea creation and design, and then in the marketing and distribution, leveraging their skills much in the way that Bose does, but on a much smaller scale. As these companies grow, they add employees to fill their expanding needs.

So while we've lost jobs from the manufacturing sector, we've created new ones, albeit these new jobs require new skills and expertise. The challenge the developed world faces is to provide the education to retrain those whose jobs have moved offshore so that they can fill the needs of the newly created positions.

With regard to quality, there are plenty of Chinese-made products of dubious quality marketed under unknown names. But look on the label of almost every product from the market leaders, such as computers, cameras, televisions, DVD recorders, mobile phones, and video game machines. These are also made in China and are as high quality as those made anywhere in the world.

Steve Leveen and his wife, Lori, are co-founders of the Florida-based company, Levenger, which designs and markets highly regarded products for reading, organization, and business. Most of their products, including leather goods, wooden furniture, accessories, and writing instruments, are made in China and Taiwan. This enables them to be much more productive and create hundreds of original products each year with a staff of about 200. As a result they've grown rapidly and are opening retail stores, each of which employs American workers.

Steve told me that they were originally attracted to China for the superior quality in addition to lower manufacturing costs. Comparing Levenger goods made in Scandinavia, Germany, the United States, the United Kingdom, India, and Latin America made it clear that the skill level of the Chinese workers and the quality control practices in their factories are some of the best in the world. For Levenger, cost is not the primary reason for sourcing there.

What about the factories employing underage labor and paying them so little? With the tremendous growth, it probably still occurs in some factories but mainly in those that don't required skilled labor and are not visible to their Western customers. But in the consumer technology areas in which I've worked I've never encountered underage employees. And with so many of the factories building products for reputable Western companies, there's a concerted effort from these companies to prevent it from occurring.

The employees, who for the most part come to the factories to make money, are often from rural farms and isolated towns, days away by train. They're not being forced, but come on their own to be able to provide money for their families back home. Many of their expenses are covered while they are working. Hiring companies provide room and board and pay overtime, allowing the workers to accumulate savings. Far from being trapped by employers, workers often move from one company to another for higher salaries and better conditions. So while their rate of pay may be low by Western standards, it is high enough for workers to be able to save money, quite a distinction from the lowest paid US and European workers.

Like most things, what's behind the stereotypical image we see is a much different picture, one more balanced and more complex than what fits into a 30-second news sound bite.

A Representative List of Recommended Resources

Additional information and listings can be found on the Website
www.fromconcepttoconsumer.com

PCH International Ltd,
Jintang Street
Shenzhen, Guangdong
P.R.CHINA 518010
www.pchchinasolutions.com
+86 755 2598 8866
Engineering, manufacturing, fulfillment, logistics

Zao Technology Innovations Inc
Silicon Valley, USA / Taipei/ Shenzhen/Shanghai/Ireland
+353-87-2420244
ray@zaotech.com
www.zaotech.com
Tooling, manufacturing, product development, product
management

Ammunition LLC
1500 Sansome Street
San Francisco CA 94111
415-632-1170
brunner@ammunitiongroup.com
www.ammunitiongroup.com
Product development and industrial design

Paul Donovan Consulting

93 Claremont Avenue

Santa Clara, CA 95051

408-605-5090

Product development, program management, and electronic design

David Lee Design

107 S. Fair Oaks Avenue, Ste. 327,

Pasadena, CA 91105

626-449-1689

dleedesign@sbcglobal.net

www.davidleedesign.org

Industrial design

Gad Shaanan Design

7979 Ivanhoe Ave.

Suite 550

La Jolla, CA 92037

858-729-9951

gad@gadshaanandesign.com

www.gadshaanandesign.com

Product development and industrial design

SurfaceInk Corporation

1485 Saratoga Ave., Suite 200

San Jose, CA 95129

408-255-3070

info@surfaceink.com

www.surfaceink.com

Engineering product development

Matrix Enterprises
12310 Stowe Drive
Poway, CA 92064
858-391-2828
estewart@matrixenterprises.com
Prototyping, modeling, engineering

Function Engineering
163 Everett Avenue
Palo Alto, CA 94301
650.326.8834
info@function.com
www.function.com
Mechanical design and engineering

Digital Age Communications, Inc.
Westfield, NJ
info@digitalage.com
Retail distribution, technology marketing and sales

Martell Communications
1673 Littleton Place
Campbell, CA 95008
408-374-7420
cmartell@martellpr.com
Public relations

Media Strategies
65 Commercial Wharf
Boston, MA 02110,
617-723-4004
cdelgreco@msipr.com
Public relations

Comunicano, Inc.

1155 Camino Del Mar
Suite 512
Del Mar, CA 92014
858-523-1800
aabramson@comunicano.com
www.comunicano.com
Public relations

Creative Strategies

2105 S. Bascom Ave.
Campbell, CA 95008
info@creativestrategies.com
www.creativestrategies.com
Analyst for high technology products and markets

Index